Clothing as Devotion in Contemporary Hinduism

D0771467

Brill Research Perspectives in Religion and the Arts

Editor-in-Chief

Diane Apostolos-Cappadona (*Georgetown University*)

Associate Editors

Barbara Baert (*University of Leuven*)
S. Brent Plate (*Hamilton College, New York*)
Zhange Ni (*Virginia Tech*)

Clothing as Devotion in Contemporary Hinduism

By

Urmila Mohan

BRILL

LEIDEN | BOSTON

This paperback book edition is simultaneously published as issue 2.4 (2018) of *Brill Research Perspectives in Religion and the Arts*, DOI:10.1163/24688878-12340006.

Library of Congress Control Number: 2019947476

Typeface for the Latin, Greek, and Cyrillic scripts: "Brill". See and download: brill.com/brill-typeface.

ISBN 978-90-04-41912-4 (paperback)
ISBN 978-90-04-41913-1 (e-book)

Printed by Printforce, the Netherlands

Contents

Clothing as Devotion in Contemporary Hinduism

Urmila Mohan
University College London, U.K.
u.mohan.11@ucl.ac.uk

Abstract

In *Clothing as Devotion in Contemporary Hinduism*, Urmila Mohan explores the materiality and visuality of cloth and clothing as devotional media in contemporary Hinduism. Drawing upon ethnographic research into the global missionizing group "International Society for Krishna Consciousness" (ISKCON), she studies translocal spaces of worship, service, education, and daily life in the group's headquarters in Mayapur and other parts of India. Focusing on the actions and values of deity dress-making, devotee clothing and paraphernalia, Mohan shows how activities, such as embroidery and chanting, can be understood as techniques of spirituality, reverence, allegiance—and she proposes the new term "efficacious intimacy" to help understand these complex processes. The monograph brings theoretical advances in Anglo-European material culture and material religion studies into a conversation with South Asian anthropology, sociology, art history, and religion. Ultimately, it demonstrates how embodied interactions as well as representations shape ISKCON's practitioners as devout subjects, while connecting them with the divine and the wider community.

Keywords

Hinduism – ISKCON – India – translocal – cloth – clothing – devotion – practice – agency – phenomenology – material culture – efficacious intimacy

1   Introduction: Why Cloth and Clothing?

Religious communities use a variety of media to emphasize the importance of a transcendental reality. Rituals and religious arts of various kinds are tangible means of using materials and bodies to make the otherworldly a real, compelling experience for believers. Further, the type of materials used shapes the kind of practices that are developed and *how* religious experiences are created. Garments help to facilitate cognitive and corporeal states, such as intimacy and protection, through actions of tying, draping, and wrapping, as well as the various stages of production such as cutting, sewing, embroidering, and so on. Although there has been much research on the efficacy of cloth in different religio-cultural contexts, the importance of this material in religious practice, especially contemporary Hindu/Indic culture, deserves further study and hence forms the subject of this monograph.

In studying tenets and practices in popular Hinduism one notes an important fact about Hinduism: unlike Judaism, Christianity, and Islam it postulates no absolute distinction between human and divine beings (Fuller 2004). Material entities can be regarded as embodiments of divinity and means of transcendence and not merely as representations. Scholars have stressed the need to be critical about Orientalist constructs in Indological studies (Inden 1986; King 1999) with terms such as "Hinduism" (Lipner 1994: 1–17) applied to diverse practices and philosophies consolidated under one –ism. Influences from monotheistic religions of the Book, such as Christianity and Islam, and criticism of idolatry, including the denigration of materials/images in religion (Assmann 2011; Fleming and Mann, eds. 2014: 3–5), have also influenced the way Hindu India was studied in the past. In addition, early Indologists and orientalists, such as Max Müller (1823–1900 CE), placed Hinduism on a scale of human religious evolution from the visible to the invisible, and from the material to the spiritual (Waghorne 1994: 89), and developed a theory of language origins wherein the Aryan civilization in India (and its oral texts) was superior to the knowledge of Dravidians and other tribal groups. In keeping with perceptions of sacredness developed by Protestant Europeans in the nineteenth century, Müller incorporated a Christian goal of inward spiritual development into his studies of India and searched for an authenticity that was to be found in text and the knowledge of Brahmins (Waghorne 1994: 88–89). He sought to fashion "a purified form of Hinduism devoid of its images and idolatrous tendencies," attributing the latter to the idea that Hindus were in a state of "noble savagery" (Sugirtharajah 2003: 60). For nineteenth-century religion scholars such as Müller, the sacred was located not only along an evolutionary scale of religious thought and practice but also via what may be termed more broadly a "surface-depth ontology" (Miller 1994)[1] with an emphasis on inner reality as spiritual essence.

---

1   This term is invoked in the context of Trinidadian clothing style where what is on the body's surface is given much importance as an indication of the true self. Miller contrasts this

The views briefly summarized above also influenced Indian self-perceptions within a British colonial context, provoking reactions such as the self-conscious articulation of a Hindu reformist and sectarian identity by religious leaders in the nineteenth and twentieth centuries. Part of this response was the codification of Hindu thought in the form of texts or exegesis of existing texts. This systematization has understandably influenced the contemporary practices of Hindu groups wherein theologians focus more on the role of scripture and the way philosophical concepts have to be negotiated in daily practice rather than the manner in which devotees rely on the nondiscursive efficacy of materials and actions. By tracing the history of approaches toward Hinduism and materiality and combining it with ethnographic reflections from my study of a global Hindu group (International Society for Krishna Consciousness, or ISKCON), this monograph emphasizes the realm of the bodily *and* material, surface and depth, to contest the long-lasting and still prevalent emphasis on inner essences as seats of Hindu spirituality and religiosity. Although limited to a specific sect of Vaishnavism and invoking aspects of sectarian philosophy, my study moves away from situating devotion in scriptural knowledge and employs a praxeological and phenomenological lens to explore deity dressmaking and devotional clothing as practices that "make" objects as well as devout subjects. As such, this monograph brings theoretical advances in Anglo-European material culture and material religion studies into a conversation with South Asian anthropology, sociology, art history, and religion.

With an intimate role as mediators of inner and outer states, cloth invokes cultural and cosmological values of the Hindu/Indic body in relation to the environment, and clothing is neither just adornment or metaphor of power and authority but "a medium through which substances can be transferred" (Cohn 1989: 312–313). As a container of "bio-moral energy" (Bayly 1986: 302) in Indic society, cloth and its properties do not merely surface the body but transmit the spirit and substance of the wearer. They possess a "magical or 'transformative' use" that is perceived to change "the moral and physical being of the wearer/recipient ... by the innate qualities of the cloth or the spirit and substance" contained and conveyed (ibid: 288). A similar fluid, dynamic approach to materials as mediators and containers of value and substance can be detected in the ethno-sociological categories developed by sociologists of India in the 1970s to study caste groupings.

Indian ethno-sociology arose with three methodological aims—(1) to use indigenous Indic terms as much as possible in the explication of Indian social

---

approach with a cultural mindset where what is important and real is believed to lie in some deep interior while what is on the surface is considered to be ephemeral and shallow.

systems and cultural practices, (2) to develop more general principles that pertain to all Indic society, and (3) to deparochialize Western social sciences. According to this approach, Hindus believe that a person physically inherits a "coded-substance" (Marriott 1990); that is, matter comes with morality built in. Each person's body has within it a single code, a set of rules that dictates what is appropriate for the person. The code programmed into the person's body influences the caste as *varna* or *jati*, and gender and personality. Simultaneously, actions transform the substances and codes in which they were embodied, and bodily substance and code for conduct are mutually immanent features. Transactions between people and objects, such as clothing and eating practices, constitute processes of mixing and separation (Marriott 1976: 109). Hence the belief that a South Asian's moral qualities are "altered by the changes in his body resulting from eating certain foods, engaging in certain kinds of sexual intercourse, taking part in certain ceremonies, or falling under certain other kinds of influence" (Marriott and Inden 1977: 228). Thus the practical logic that underpins life as a Hindu is that one should try to gain appropriate or "superior" coded-particles (those coming from gods or higher castes) not "worse" coded particles (those coming from lower castes or defiled persons and objects). Following Marriott's ethno-sociological initiative and theory of Indian "substance-codes," the South Asian person emerges as a fluid, loosely bounded "dividual" whose concerns with regulating interpersonal transactions are part of a constant negotiation of biological instability and moral risk. It is within this ontology of divisible bodies and materials that one might understand Hindu religious concepts such as *karma* (action) and *dharma* (moral-religious order, coherence) and practices such as *darshan* (worshipful gaze) and *bhakti* (devotion).

By emphasizing the physical and metaphysical uses of cloth in an Indian context, one blurs not only the domains of the "natural" and the "moral"; categories of the "religious," "secular," and "political" are also blurred. For instance, by using ideas of ornament as religiosity, Waghorne (1994) relates a nineteenth-century South Indian king's ceremonial meeting room (*durbar*) with his predecessor's role in religious ritual. She further connects the *durbar* to a contemporaneous Victorian mantlepiece in the United Kingdom with its assortment of world objects from different parts of the British empire. By situating her study against the historical background of the Raj (British rule), Hindu courtly tradition and the connections created between India and Britain, Waghorne argues that ornament *is* ontology, bringing into existence both the power of the South Indian king as well as the British colonial powers. Ornament, Waghorne argues, conferred vitality and life on the king's body in the Southern kingdom of Pudukkottai, and mythology and history are a vehicle for the embodiment of the divine in the body of the king. By invoking the role of "ornament as ontology" Waghorne also provides a meta-commentary on the importance of understanding religious and political history, and the way religion was manifested/understood in colonial India. Such an approach can be brought into studying contemporary India as well, for instance, in relating the practices and beliefs of contemporary Hindu sects to colonial influences in the nineteenth century. (This issue is explored in more detail later.)

A discussion of cloth invokes not only the use of materials as bodily ornamentation (*alankar*) but the intimacy of materials in general, that is, the role of cloth in making the divine body of the deity/king as well as the human body of the devotee/subject. By coming into close contact with the body during processes of worship and other "devotional" practices (such as dressmaking and chanting), cloth and clothing enable us to explore the role of bodily processes through the lens of beliefs, practice, aesthetics, and emotions. For example, when speaking of their spiritual experiences, Hindu devotees may refer to a "higher taste," or relish, of an experience called *rasa*, a common term in Indian aesthetics. In Sanskrit *rasa* means "sap," "juice," or "fluid essence" and invokes a transcendental experience, specifically termed *bhakti rasa*, whereby the devotee is connected to the divine sublime through a form of sensory appreciation.

Rasa is also an Indian aesthetic concept that describes a flavorful essence or the relish of a particular experience or interaction (Schwartz 2004: 7–10). The mythic-historical figure Bharata is accredited with writing, approximately two millennia ago, a text on dramatic and aesthetic theory titled *Natyasastra* (Vatsyayan 1996). The eight *rasas* (*shringar, hasya, karuna, raudra, veer, bhayanak, vibhatsa, adbhuta*) correspond to eight *bhavas*. *Bhavas* are intransitive properties, such as the sweetness of a plum, whereas the *rasas* are the corresponding experiences that activate the property, such as tasting the sweetness. In the tenth century, Abhinavagupta, the most important commentator on Bharata, added the ninth transcendental *rasa*, called *shanta* (peace or bliss), which is considered to be a perfect mix of all the other *rasas*. The term *bhava* is etymologically related to the term *anubhav*, whose meanings include "direct perception," "knowledge derived from personal observation or experiment," and "an external manifestation or indication of a feeling by appropriate symptoms, such as by look, gesture, etc."[2] According to this etymological relationship, material and sensory entities on the temple altar, such as decoration and clothing, help to activate and relate a devotee's *anubhav* to his or her emotional and spiritual states.

---

2 See https://dsalsrv04.uchicago.edu/cgi-bin/app/apte_query.py?page=101, last accessed 16 April 2019.

In the fifteenth century, Rupa Gosvami, the great Gaudiya theologian and companion of the saint and mystic Chaitanya (1486–1533 CE), expanded on the transcendental and salvational aspects of aesthetic experience to author the *Bhaktirasamritasindhu*,[3] in which the spiritual world is an eternal drama or performance of the love of the deity Krishna, an incarnation of Vishnu, and his consort Radha. *Bhakti*, or devotional love, was the only real practice that could awaken *rasa* as *bhava*, or mood, by enabling the devotee to discover his or her true identity in relationship to Krishna. Accordingly, certain new *rasas* that would enable a devotee to perform a role—*dasya* (relationship of servant to master), *sakhya* (friendship), and *vatsalya* (parental affection)—were extolled over the comic, tragic, and horrific. Whatever the role, the ultimate devotional goal was learning how to utilize *raga* (creative-emotive aesthetics) to elicit the *rasa* of divine love for Krishna or, for that matter, any deity within the Vaishnav *bhakti* tradition. In *bhakti* sects such as ISKCON's Gaudiya Vaishnavism the emphasis on *raga* is balanced with the knowledge of *vidhi/vaidhi* (rule-based, normative) devotion. Emotions saturate material practices such that *raga* and *vidhi*, the creative and the injunctive, are equally important in worshipping the deity.

2   Deity Worship and *Darshan*

The issue of how a stone or metal figure can be a divine person has perplexed and engaged scholars of religion with a history in Western attitudes toward idolatry, including the denigration of materials in religion (Fleming and Mann, eds. 2014: 3–5, Mann 2014). More recently scholars have posited Hindu deity worship as a case for the recognition of intimacy between the human and the divine through the relationship of flesh and stone, that is, in the form of *archa avatara* (worshipable incarnations) and *murtis* (sentient images) (Waghorne, Cutler, and Narayanan, eds. 1985). These are rendered in materials, such as stone and metal, and are subjected to embodied worship (*puja*) by devotees. Although ritual labor is required to suitably install and worship such artefacts, they are considered self-manifestations (*swarup*) of the deity and not just products of human activity.

Although deity worship is by no means the central principle of all "Hinduism," it is nonetheless a popular one, including within global Hindu groups, such as ISKCON, that have strong roots in India and incorporate

---

3   Republished in 2003.

the devotional practices of other Krishna temples, such as those in Puri, Vrindavan, and Nathdwara. The Hindu deity is akin to royalty and the temple is his or her court. Just like royalty, the deity uses a pool of ritual paraphernalia and is referred to as king (*raja*) as well as universal lord (*bhagwan*) and the devotee assumes the role of the dependent and server. As part of a deity's *prasad*, or grace, material (whether clothing, food, flowers) consumed by the deity is believed to have been ontologically transformed, carrying auspiciousness for a devotee-beneficiary through its very contact and substance. In this context, "the physical is valued because it is capable of transformation ... the categories of material and spiritual do not function in an inverse relationship but rather function in the same way that materials matter to the artist" (Waghorne 1994: 257).

Traditionally, notions of embodiment and life were incorporated into the deity figure through ritualized means of production as well as installation. For instance, the sculpting of deity figures for temples as well as the architecture of the temples themselves follows proportions stipulated in the ancient "Shilpa Shastra" ("artist" or "architect" and "knowledge" or "science"). According to instructions from the Shilpa Shastra canon, the idealized human body acts as a source of religio-magical power and measurement, with the ratio of the body's various parts standardized and translated into iconography, architecture, and sculpture. A set of instruction in scriptures ranging from the eighth century to the seventeenth century was used in the twentieth century by an artist and scholar to make clay figures, later compared with the folk artform of temporary unbaked clay figures for the festival of Durga Puja in West Bengal (Varma 1970). This comparison showed compelling similarities in the making process. Regardless of the Hindu sect involved, the process of making the deity image (*murti*) is central, since it is only once the image is made that it can be rendered sentient and worshipable.

Part of the similarity between clay modeled forms and stone sculptures used in temples or rituals is the incorporation of beliefs in *nadi*, or the pulse of life force, whereby energy circulates through the body through a network of pulses. In a temple context, a life force must be incorporated during the consecration of the figure in a ritual called *prana pratistha* ("life force positioning"). For instance, at the time of consecration, a *murti* in a South Indian temple is marked with a series of *nadi*; a string is tied to a point/pulse on the *murti*'s wrist to transmit the energy of installation rituals and thus give it life (Waghorne 2004: 192). After installation, as several authors have demonstrated, actions of worship (feeding, bathing, singing) keep the sentient deity appeased. Keeping this in mind, deity clothing activities could be considered part of a temple's everyday rituals, especially in those places where the deity's outfits are changed several times a day. Further, rituals such as *darshan*, the exchange of embodied gaze between devotee and deity, are related to the appeal of the altar and gain popularity in part because of the deity's attractive appearance.

The concept of *darshan* in Hindu worship has been studied by numerous scholars from various perspectives, mostly as an exchange of perspectives between devotee and deity or, in some cases, between human beings in a hierarchical relationship (Babb 1981; Bhatti and Pinney 2011; Eck 1981; Gell 1998: 116–117; Miles 1998: 169; Pinney 2004). The meanings of *darshan* include seeing, exhibiting, teaching, observation, perception, experiencing, discernment, understanding, and philosophical system (Monier-Williams 2005 [1872]: 470–471). Through these meanings we can understand that *darshan* covers two types of "seeing"—that is, both as physical gaze as well as metaphysical insight. The process of visuality is not just a means to imbibe the deity's benevolent gaze but to substantially transform oneself through a partaking of the deity's substance. The deity graces the devotee with the ability to see/feel the divine image, and the devotee-recipient is transformed. Conversely, the devotee is attracted to the temple by love for the deity and a sensorial experience that is heightened by its beauty. Sensory intimacy with the deity involves a human intake of transformative substance from the deity and is hence a practice that creates a sense impression and forms the devotee. By interacting visually with a superior being, the devotee hopes to ultimately become part of a superior way of seeing and knowing. *Darshan* can also extend to touching the deity with one's hands (*sparsha*), touching the limbs of one's body to establish the presence of deities (*nyasha*), hearing the sacred sound of mantras (*shravana*) and music, as well as inhaling the perfume of flowers and burning incense. The hierarchical emphasis on the transformatory aesthetics and experience of *darshan* is resonated in the practice of *prasad* ("grace" in Sanskrit) and the consumption of food, flowers, and clothing formerly offered to the deity.[4]

Phenomenologists have explored the subject as relating to the world through the body and the body as the "being-in-the-world" of the subject where the world is a field of awareness and meaning. Merleau-Ponty (2012 [1945]) and Csordas (ed. 1994, 1997) continued this program of investigation with Merleau-Ponty more on the philosophical side and Csordas more on the

---

4   In a culture where taking somebody else's leftovers (*jhuta*) can be highly polluting and dangerous, the voluntary consumption of *prasad* expresses the preference for superior substances such as those associated with the deity that will positively "contaminate" and transform the devotee.

anthropological side.[5] Following the legacy of the phenomenologist Maurice Merleau-Ponty (2012 [1945]), the art historian David Morgan (2010) stressed the value of embodiment in the study of material culture and religion. He noted that practices relate the individual body to the social body "as a larger version of the group and the self that envisions it," discerned by "feeling, sensation, and imagination." The anthropologist Alfred Gell, who otherwise had little interest in Hinduism, used the example of the sentient deity figure (*murti*) to explain his concept of external and internal agency and how such an otherwise inanimate entity is believed to be animated. Gell (1998: 134) proposed a combination of external and internal agency whereby the external kind is induced by praxis, such as acts of feeding, bathing, and dressing, and the internal kind is induced by the belief that the deity possesses a mind and has intentionality. He theorized the transformative agency of artefacts and proposed the term "enchantment" (1992) to describe the dynamic by which human and artefactual agency are enmeshed in a network of intentionalities, including the production and use of objects.

In the case of Hindu groups that practice *bhakti* (devotion) and *sewa* (service), embodiment may be thought of as the devotee's sense of relationship to the deity, accessed and practiced through the shared aesthetics and culture of services such as *shringar* (costume and decoration), food and music, and shared worship experiences such as *darshan*. Here, a praxeological approach may be useful in considering religion as a "culture of motricity" (Warnier 2007: 1, fn. 1). The Matière à Penser (MAP)[6] group emphasizes that the two entities—body and material—cannot be separated in practice (Gowlland 2011; Mohan and Warnier 2017; Naji and Douny 2009). Combining Gell's, Morgan's, and MAP's ideas on agency, embodiment, and praxis, one can take devotees' beliefs seriously as well as explore how *murtis* come to be accorded such animated power and efficacy by their human devotees; that is, *how* do worship practices transform the body and mind, for instance, through dressing, dressmaking, and chanting to create and shape devotees?

---

5   Csordas (1990: 33) takes Durkheim (2008 [1912]) to task for making society the force that defines religious power and seeks this force in embodied experience, as when a thought occurs to a person or there is an experience of being controlled by another force. Although Csordas observes that physiological theories may provide accounts of mechanisms, such as trance and catharsis, he does not explore *how* the former may help us understand cultural expressions (Csordas in Strathern 1996: 180).

6   For the basic ideas and examples of application of MAP, combining Foucault's (1988) technologies of self and Mauss's (2006 [1935]) techniques of self, see Mohan, Urmila, and Laurence Douny, eds. 2020. *The Material Subject*.

3   ISKCON as Translocal Hindu Group

From the twentieth century onward the borders of relationships in Hindu groups have been increasingly defined by a complex global network of relational and contextual factors wherein it is the phenomenological quality of the network's social life that aids in translocal flows of Hinduism and not simply the political concept of the nation and its geographic borders. The approach of analyzing globalization as a shifting topography of "scapes" (Appadurai 1996) was extended to include the "religioscape" (Dwyer 2004: 196), a concept that encourages us to study the phenomenon of translocal Hindu flows through the ways in which people emplace themselves in new locales. Simultaneously, the devotional modalities of *bhakti* and Hindu deity worship have proven to be experientially compelling, transcending national borders and boundaries, and they seem to follow Csordas's (2009: 1) definition of the globalization of religions as "transnational transcendence."

Concerns of inalienability are deemed to rarely lessen the dissemination of Hinduism, because practices are "portable" (Froystad in Csordas 2009: 285), and religion "territorialises" (Appadurai 1996: 38) by forming religioscapes of phenomenological and inter-subjective relationships. In parallel to these developments, there has been a surge of academic interest in the importance of lived experience in Hinduism through an interest in "decolonizing methodologies," with some scholars warning that the "privileging of written texts and beliefs" had led to the marginalization of other ways of knowing and transmitting beliefs (Narayanan 2003: 516).

While noting the importance of the nation in defining "Hinduism," this monograph focuses on translocality in the study of ISKCON, where deity dressing and devotee clothing practices illustrate how the group relies on individual, local nodes situated within the geographical and cultural system. The ethnographic research for this monograph is drawn from approximately a year of fieldwork (2012–2013) in the Chandrodaya temple, ISKCON's spiritual headquarters in Mayapur, West Bengal, India, as well as visits to various centres in India (Bengaluru, Chennai, Mumbai). As a universalizing group with roots, and now a substantial presence in India, ISKCON presents a complex terrain that speaks to the role of Hinduism in contemporary India as well as in the world. The group is part of a disparate collection of Hindu organizations, such as Ramakrishna Mission, Swaminarayan, Satya Sai Baba, and others, that came out of different contexts but are united in projecting an acceptable face of Hinduism and have branches worldwide. Earlier concerns about ISKCON's authenticity have now been replaced by an acceptance of the group as one that was founded by an Indian guru and that is a successful disseminator of

devotion or *bhakti*.[7] Hindu identity is no longer just a question of a geographi-
cally bound Indian identity, and "diasporic environments have become fertile
sites for ... Hindus to present themselves as champions of Hindu dharma"
(Sugirtharajah 2003: 134) as well as revitalizing and reaffirming Hindu religion
and culture.

ISKCON's formulation of *bhakti* as Krishna Consciousness or Krishna-
centered-ness must be situated against its Gaudiya (Bengali) Vaishnav roots as
well as the history of Hindu reformist/revitalization groups. The group affirms
a devotional form of worship centered on Krishna, "which the nineteenth-
century Protestant orientalists and missionaries derided and for whom, as we
have seen, any expression of ardent or ecstatic devotion, *bhakti*, was a mark of
effeminacy" (Sugirtharajah 2003: 136). The various *bhakti* institutions of North
India divide along the *saguna/nirguna* line—that is, accepting a god who is *saguna* (with qualities) and is to be worshipped by means of sentient images and
a god who is *nirguna* (without qualities). The Gaudiya *sampraday* (tradition)
is an example of the *saguna* tradition, although, in practice, the difference
between *saguna/nirguna* is often blurred (Hawley 1995, 2015; Prentiss 1999:
21). Given the inbuilt plurality of *bhakti* traditions in India, one must know
ISKCON's history to understand its type of devotionalism.

In the case of Gaudiya Vaishnavism, the public cult of Vaishnavism in Bengal
suffered from withdrawal of state patronage under the medieval Turko-Afghan
sultans. It next appeared as a "popular devotional movement unmediated by
priestly rituals or court patronage" (Eaton 1993: 110) with vernacular literature
glorifying the various incarnations of Vishnu. The love of Radha, Krishna's female consort, for Krishna became the central theme of Bengali *bhakti* and crys-
tallized around the saint and mystic Chaitanya in the fifteenth century. Initial
resistance came not from Muslims but from Brahmin supporters of other cults.
Indeed, this new Krishna literature was partly patronized by the Muslim court
at Gaur (a city on the present-day Bangladesh-India border), and, under the
Hussain Shahi rulers, Chaitanya Vaishnavism in the sixteenth century provided
a limited integrative space for people of different religions and status through
its advocacy of *madhurya*—a gentle, humane kind of devotion. In Gaudiya
Vaishnav *bhakti*, the divine is a person and religion is about forming a personal
relationship with Krishna that will ultimately be emotionally fulfilling and so-
teriologically rewarding. The importance of devotional union is built into the
doctrine of ISKCON; following Krishna Dasa Kaviraj's *Chaitanya Charitamrita*,

---

7   Although scholars such as Sander and Cavallin (2015: 1756) may speak of ISKCON's "return" to
    India, the term should be considered indicative of wider recognition in India rather than a
    previous separation from the country.

authored in the sixteenth century, the saint Chaitanya was worshipped as an incarnation of both Krishna and his female consort Radha (Dimock 1999).

The early modern period in Bengal was also a time of change and upheaval with struggles for power between the beleaguered Mughal empire, the semi-independent Nawabs, and local *zamindars* (landowners tasked with revenue collection). The kingdom of Nadiya under Krishnachandra (1728–1782 CE) rose and fell with the changing socio-economic and political environment. The king lived through a tumultuous period that saw him first preside over a splendid court and then the decline and ruin of Nadiya, brought about by a combination of factors (Lyons 2009). Changes in the celebration of Durga Puja at this time can be traced to the king's supernatural experiences under stressful circumstances with the creation of a new goddess, Jagaddhatri, subsequently adopted by various communities and whose fluidity of iconography and worship can be traced up to today. On witnessing the festivities of such events, foreign observers of the eighteenth and nineteenth centuries concluded that "Bengalis were insincere, and that the entire spectacle was being staged to impress their peers and the Company elite" (ibid: 264). However, the landholding families of Bengal maintained their strong belief in the importance of proper ritual worship and goddesses such as Jagaddhatri since it was connected to their faith as well as being an indigenous response to global historical forces that caused the decline of the local aristocracy.

Against this backdrop of religious and political change in Bengal, ISKCON's history is directly tied with events of the nineteenth century, when religious conscientization, or *sudhi*, was introduced into Hinduism as part of a "renaissance." Further, it was during this time that an Enlightenment conception of religion partly influenced by Western Orientalists (with notions of linear history and progress) was adopted by Hindu thinkers such as Rammohan Roy, Dayananda Saraswati, Vivekananda, Radhakrishnan, and others. Hinduism was conceived and presented as an organized religion with an organized priesthood and a church with a congregation and missionaries to aid proselytization. The creation of the *bhadralok* (genteel middle class) in nineteenth-century Bengal could also be considered an example of a type of indigenous response to colonialism and Christianity. Spiritual guides of the *bhadralok* included its members, such as the bureaucrat-turned-theologian Kedarnath Dutta (1838–1914 CE), later known as Bhaktivinoda Thakur, who used *bhakti* to revitalize Gaudiya Vaishnavism and form the monastic order of the Gaudiya *Math*, or monastery.

The nineteenth century was a period that also marked the introduction and expansion of print technology in India. Print marked the shift from an emphasis on experiencing the text through its performative orality and aurality to the

commentarial tradition accompanied by silent, individual reading and reflec-
tion (Fuller 2005b). Simultaneously, texts such as the *Ramcharitmanas* continued to be part of North Indian performative traditions (Lutgendorf 1991).
In this changing milieu, the theological and exegetical dimensions of Hindu
scriptures became increasingly important as a domain of critical concern for
reformers such as Bhaktivinoda. Print allowed Bhaktivinoda to reason and dis-
seminate his particular understanding of *bhakti* and divinity (Bhatia 2017: 128).
For instance, the *Bhagavata Purana*, also known as the *Srimad Bhagavatam*,
was interpreted and standardized for readers as sacred scripture (*shastra*) and
not just as stories of the life of Krishna to be borrowed for performative and
literary purposes. Characteristically the authoritative, systematizing product
of Brahmin authors, *shastra*, according to Lutgendorf (1991: 342), had never en-
joyed mass appeal in India, since it largely seemed disconnected from the (cha-
otic) activities of the world. Text as *shastra* is a distinct modality of religious
propagation that in a modern Hindu reform context becomes self-consciously
doctrinal and ideological (Laine 2010: 242).[8] Simultaneously, materials and
practices in ISKCON have acted as means of proselytization, especially in the
context of deity worship in temples. Indeed, the complementary role of scripture and deity worship can be seen in the logo of the Gaudiya *math* (monastery) in Bengal, where religious practice is symbolized by images such as
books, deity images (*murtis*), drum, printing press, religious mark (*tilak*), and
the figure of the ecstatic, dancing medieval saint Chaitanya.

The goal for Bhaktivinoda was not only to reveal the truths of Gaudiya
Vaishnavism but also to make Krishna (and the saint Chaitanya) entities who
could hold their own in front of rationalists, Westerners, and the English-
educated (Bhatia 2017: 122; Lipner 2006: 102; Nandy 1983: 24). Bhaktivedanta
Swami Prabhupada (1896–1977 CE) was a disciple of the son of Bhaktivedanta
named Bhaktisiddhanta Saraswati (1874–1937 CE). Prabhupada (formerly
known as Abhay Charan De) was initiated by Bhaktisiddhanta in 1933, and
his goal was to impart his teacher's message to the West such that it would
ultimately come back to revitalize the East. The incorporation of ISKCON in
New York in 1966 could thus be considered an outcome of Bhaktisiddhanta's
missionary vision and, as devotees claim, Chaitanya's missionizing desires
as well, casting a predictive power retrospectively on the saint. Although
the term "member" is still under debate, for our purposes ISKCON now has

---

8   Here I highlight the various kinds of texts and the reformist emphasis on the prescriptive,
    doctrinal text. Performative uses of texts might be said to exist even within ISKCON through
    the example of chanting mantras.

approximately one million members globally, including at least 270,000 registered life members in India[9] and over 400 temples worldwide.

It has been argued that, historically, in the absence of formal conversion, educational practices had early on become ways for people to transform themselves into Hindus (Sharma 2011: 107). ISKCON takes on attributes of both an educational group and a religious corporation and combines them to situate itself as a modern missionary organization. It preaches a universalizing form of Hinduism and a revitalized caste system (*varnashram dharma*) in which anybody can become a Brahmin as long as they are qualified to be initiated through a program of immersion, affiliation, and study. ISKCON does not do away with the caste system but adapts it. It argues that caste is not inherited but is a matter of transformation of substance and that anybody can refine themselves through devotional life. Spiritual merit does not accrue from birth but from the transformative practice of *bhakti* yoga and one's mental, emotional, and physical surrender to Krishna. The term "Krishna Consciousness" refers to the process of awakening the devotee's awareness of the true reality of the material world as illusion (*maya*) and the true goal of soteriological union with Krishna to avoid the cycle of life, death, and reincarnation (*samsara*). In a seeming paradox, these transcendental values are sustained by the heightened sensuality and materiality of deity-worship practices and their use in attracting and sustaining devotees.

As we shall see in the forthcoming sections, materials and the values and discourses that surround bodies and objects help to shape devotional subjects. However, with a few exceptions that use a phenomenological and affective analysis of music, food, space, and worship,[10] existing scholarship on ISKCON and Gaudiya Vaishnavism[11] is silent on the issue of materiality. A significant part of scholarship on ISKCON (including recent works by devotees) focuses

---

9   This is based on paid membership figures for metro areas and towns in India as of 2013. Itis far less than the number of people who are informally affiliated with or initiated by ISKCON. The term "member" is debatable also because it is used to refer to a range of associations from a weekend temple visitor to someone who is officially registered. Membership is also affected by schisms such as the formation of a temple in Bengaluru that has 40,000 life members. For our purposes, the Bengaluru temple could also be considered part of the Hare Krishna group, bringing the total official membership figure in India to approximately 270,000.

10   See Brown 2012; King 2012; Sarbadhikary 2015; Valpey 2006.

11   See Bromley and Shinn, eds. 1989; Brooks 1989, 1990; Fuller 2005a; Holdrege 2014; Nye 2001; Rochford 2007; Zaidman 1997.

on the history and formation of the group in the West and in India.[12] While drawing on insights in this body of scholarship, this monograph differs by exploring the making of the devotional subject through a direct, in-depth observation of materials, techniques, and practices.

4   Multi-sensorial Worship Experience

In the context of the ocular exchange (*darshan*) between deity and devotee the aesthetics of the altar are key to the creation of an elaborate visual spectacle that attracts a devotee's eye and orients his or her body toward the altar. As an example, let us consider the altar in the ISKCON temple in Mayapur, West Bengal, where the deities Radha and Krishna (in the form of Radha-Madhava, Figure 1) are worshipped along with the eight Astasakhis (main *gopis*, or milkmaids), five large figures of Panchatattva (Chaitanya and his associates), and a separate shrine dedicated to the ferocious form of the half-lion, half-human Narasimha with his boy-devotee Prahlad.[13]

In the temple the *darshanic* experience is heightened by an altar that celebrates Krishna as a dancing deity with the play of light on glittering sequins, shimmering silks, and the flow of long garlands and draped fabric (Figure 1). Terms such as opulent and effulgent are associated with the physical properties of the deity garments as well as with the deity's qualities of absolute intelligence, perfection, and beauty. Worship practices, such as the waving of lamps in front of the deities, help to reiterate the connection between sight, light, and enlightenment. The ambient light (or lack of it) also influences the mood in the temple—for example, the deity at a predawn worship appears more radiant because of the minimal lighting in the temple. (Devotees also describe this as the most intimate, potent, and auspicious *darshan* of the day.) In addition to light, color is a metaphysical entity that aids the mutually embodied, transformative sight exchange between deity and devotee in the temple or between a guru and a devotee.

Following ISKCON's Bengali Vaishnav theology the human hand is engaged through personalized service (*sewa*) and worship of the deity. *Bhakti*,

---

12   These works are by devotees who either are academics or provide the insights of members through collaborations between academics and devotees. See Bryant and Ekstrand, eds. 2004; Dasa 1985; Dwyer and Cole, eds. 2007; Goswami 2012; Rochford 1985; Sardella 2013.

13   In the Hindu pantheon, Narasimha is a figure of liminality that exists between spaces and between times, and so his images are placed in locations that are similarly in between, for example, in entryways. Narasimha is a ferocious deity who saved his boy-devotee Prahlad by killing the boy's persecutor and father, the demon Hiranyakashipu.

FIGURE 1   Radha-Madhava altar on the festival of *Janmashtami* (Krishna's birthday).
MAYAPUR, 2012. IMAGE BY AUTHOR

or devotional love for the deity, is most apparent in the temple as *murti-sewa*, or service of the deity image, which shows caring for the *murtis* as if they were sentient beings. The beautiful altar, priestly attendance, *abhishek* (bathing of the deity in different substances), and sumptuous *bhogas* (food offerings) for the deities help to create a mood of festivity and opulence and are believed to please the deities such that they respond by being "merciful" and grant the desires of their worshippers. As the protocol accorded a royal person directs, Krishna is welcomed and refreshed, and every morning he is bathed, clothed, and ornamented.

Whereas the traditional model of the Hindu temple would have the devotee moving from public to more secluded spaces and finally into the *sanctum sanctorum* (also known as the womb chamber, or *garba gruha*), the proselytizing ISKCON temple has large open spaces for congregation. Such gathering spaces facilitate large crowds and devotional singing and dancing (*sankirtan*), a feature of Gaudiya Vaishnavism. Ghosh (2005) analyzes terracotta Vaishnav temples in Bengal that were built during the seventeenth and eighteenth centuries and argues that distinctive temple architecture was created by merging features of mosques, such as the Islamic prayer hall, with thatched huts to form the double-storey temple. This new type of temple acted as an "object of translation" (Flood 2009) that met the needs of changing political patronage and worship culture that served the newly developing religious tradition of

Chaitanya Vaishnavism. Devotees who wished to energetically celebrate and praise the deities through singing and dancing could now use the main space of the temple and bring together large groups of people. Although scholars have focused on such activities as "spiritual," one should also explore how other seemingly secular activities prepare the devotee for *darshan*. For example, a suitable mood of worship is imposed through injunctions and practices that control the devotee's body. This control is exercised by what the temple may codify both administratively as well as theologically as the official mood of worship. In ISKCON, although the primary deities are clearly worshipped *as* Radha-Krishna, they are approached in the more formal mood of service of the deity Vishnu and his female consort Lakshmi. The emphasis on respect extends beyond ritual considerations to the numerous rules that govern the entry of pilgrims into the temple, especially into those with large pilgrim populations, such as the Mayapur temple.

Since ISKCON practices are fairly standardized one can assume that in most urban temples in India guards monitor the entry of pilgrims, who must first divest themselves of items such as luggage, electronic goods, phones, and footwear. Increasingly, devotees can take formal tours of temples and, in some cases, view museum-like displays that illustrate the history of the group and the hagiography of Gaudiya Vaishnav saints. While leaving these "tourist-devotees" are encouraged to exit the temple through the giftshop, a place where they can buy souvenirs and books and thereby help support the temple. The regulated temple with its emphasis on queues, barriers, security checks, cleanliness, and decorum points to the kind of modern pilgrim envisioned. It is also part of a larger worship culture in India where, in general, the theistic (*saguna bhakti*) tradition of popular Hinduism has become increasingly public and ostentatious and must be related to emerging forms of religious consumption (Nanda 2011: 74). For example, the Akshardham Cultural Complex (ACC), a structure built by the Swaminarayan Vaishnav sect in Delhi, is part of the phenomena accompanying the growth of the Indian middle class and their new needs and aspirations (Brosius 2010). Swaminarayan is considered an incarnation of Krishna, and the ACC site acts both as a pilgrimage and tourist spot.

In addition to the ingestion of the deity's grace through forms of *prasad*, the body's kinesthetic system is engaged through such practices as dancing, prostration, circumambulation, and rolling on the floor. In particular, the ecstatic, congregational worship of Gaudiya Vaishnavism highlights the use of the devotional body as a sensual entity that helps elicit spontaneous emotions and states. Energy in its various forms (sound, motion, vibration) is conceptualized as a vehicle of animating divine presence. One can find numerous instances in the Gaudiya Vaishnav text *Chaitanya Charitamrita* where the saint Chaitanya's ecstatic convulsions are described using such terms as jumping, rolling, roaring, crying, perspiring, shivering, and having goose bumps (Dimmock 1999: 375). These physical and emotional manifestations are considered transcendental symptoms of divine contact and help to relate the natural and supernatural on a phenomenological and sensory register. It is not coincidental that religious subjects use the analogies of forces, such as electricity and magnetism, to invoke divine power and causality. Pinney (1997: 166–167) narrates how, in the case of one of his Hindu informants, the efficacy of a mantra is compared to the process of turning on a tubelight—a press of a switch that ensures a flow of electricity. Pinney's informant describes it as a process that is *bina vishvas*, that is, it does not require belief in the deity, just a mechanical recitation of the sounds of the mantra. In ISKCON's practice of *bhakti*, by contrast, the "flow of electricity" (at least for a neophyte) requires belief as intentionality, emotion, and effort to transform body and mind.[14] In the Mayapur guesthouse, signs placed on the doors ask guests to conserve electricity, since it is "Krishna's energy." Such practices and reminders of the omniscience of Krishna shift the devotee closer to the deity and create a sense of intimacy through emotive, aesthetic appeal. In most contexts the boon or result that devotees hope for is not a miracle but a feeling of intimacy that makes divinity palpable and senseable and moves the devotee closer to the deity along the emotive-aesthetic path of *raga*.

Temple worship is an activity that involves immersion in a sensorial experience through coordinated public performances of praise and celebration while at the same time allowing devotees to develop personal relationships with the deity. Vision is not a high-order, intellectual sense but one that is imbricated in a dynamic sensorium where perception is grounded in motion. Learning how to see and feel the deity is a means of knowing the deity and is synonymous with enlightenment and transformation. It is also part of how one is oriented and moved toward the deity. This sensorial and emotional experience thus contributes to the felt-life of the devotee and the perception of the deity as real. Religion, to follow Mauss's (2006 [1935]) famous essay titled "Techniques of the Body," could be considered the ultimate bodily technique, involving actions that are both traditional and efficacious. Here the author (ibid: 90) asks about the descending *kabyle* (Algerian Berber) slipper-wearer: "How can he keep his feet without the slippers coming off?" Warnier (2009: 7) answers with

---

14 This comparison, while necessary for this paper, can be further nuanced. The informant glosses over the fact that along with efficacious sounds there is indeed a need for belief. Although the devotee (or the recipient of his knowledge) does not have to believe, the guru's role as intermediary between deity and devotee is essential to finding the right mantra. In effect, the guru has already "turned on" the switch.

the reasoning that the slippers have been incorporated into his motor habits by apprenticeship and that the slippers have become part of his body-schema, or *Körperschema*. The concept of body-schema was first proposed by Schilder (1950 [1935]: 11) to suggest "the picture of our own body which we form in our mind." The body extends beyond its coetaneous envelope, and its schema is composed of both precepts and images of internal and external stimuli. Following Schilder, the body's schema or self-image is constantly changing depending on the physical incorporation or excorporation of objects. The resulting self and its corporeal boundary is related to the formation of the subject through internal and external forces such as emotions, perceptions, senses, and actions. In the context of ISKCON, devotees seem to literally shape themselves through worship by using paraphernalia and making clothing for their deities within the paradigm of *bhakti sewa*. A similar approach could be used to explore devotional activity in other Hindu groups to understand how the bodily and material are imbricated and thereby how devotional subjectivity is created.

5   Clothing the Deities: Toward an ISKCON Style

Cloth is multivocal and can be approached as having not just agency but also affinity: as being an entity that enters into different relations of materials, substances, and actions within Hindu cosmology—flexible enough that it is part of the world's *maya*, or illusion, but also physically enabling a sanctified life on earth or the promise of salvation. Cloth mediates notions of purity (*shudh*) and auspiciousness (*shubh*) that are important in the study of Hindu practices as relational categories and meaningful in their variable intersection. In everyday speech *shubh* applies to those acts that are conducive to joy and well-being and qualifies signs (*lakshana*) that indicate those states (Madan 1985). For a Hindu devotee everything related to a specific deity, including the associated materials, could be regarded as auspicious and pure. When deities are dressed to appear regal and powerful one could argue that the physical signs of these traits—such as beauty, grace, splendor, and luster—are part of divine auspiciousness as embedded in the garment's aesthetics and materials.

Auspiciousness may also be related to the types of actions performed by makers as well as the purity of materials being used. For example, the *Padma Saliyars* (a weaving community in Tamil Nadu, India) are not just makers and sellers of textiles but also providers of "auspicious cloths" (Kawlra 2005) for people and temples. Studying the technical and cultural aspects of sari weaving by this community demonstrates how auspiciousness is constituted in the *korvai* weaving process by creating ornamental and textural elements that come together visually and materially. There is a hierarchy of value among materials, and gold and silver are considered purest among metals, and silk is preferred to cotton. The *korvai* sari embodies auspiciousness not just through its woven form and visual effect but also by bringing together in the acts of weaving, selling, and wearing the various social, symbolic, and tempero-spatial elements that are regarded as creating auspiciousness and purity, along with their ability to influence/unmix one's bodily substance as needed in a transformative and relational manner. The sari in this case is as close as one can get to the motto of Indian ethical-aesthetic culture of being *Satyam, Shivam, Sundaram*, or good," "beautiful," and "true," and the sari's innovation and use are based on achieving and mobilizing such efficacious states.

To better understand how such auspicious qualities could be imbued in deity garments, let us turn to the concept of *alankar. Alankar* is a Sanskrit term for ornamentation and adornment that means "to make sufficient or strengthen, to make adequate" (Coomaraswamy 1939: 376–377; Dehejia 2009: 24; Gonda 1975: 256–274). *Abharan*, another Sanskrit word for adornment, means to bring near or attract through magical power (Gonda 1975: 171–177). Ornament is both attractive and protective and makes the body complete, whole, and desirable. To be without ornament is to provoke the forces of inauspiciousness and to expose oneself to danger. According to this logic, the making and assembling of the deity's adornment results in a gradual augmentation of the deity's presence and power (*shakti*). This notion of ornament as something that is vital to the artefact contradicts the idea that embellishment is superfluous.[15] Depending on the religious sect—for instance, as among Jain monks and nuns—avoidance of ornamented textiles can connote the power of austerity and devotion (Gupta 1996: 34–44).

ISKCON's deity worship is influenced by the practices of other Krishna temples, such as Shrinathji in Nathdwara, Rajasthan;[16] the various Goswami temples in Vrindavan, Uttar Pradesh;[17] and the Jagannath temple in Puri, Orissa.[18] Simultaneously, certain religious flows and associations are indicated and supported through the specific temple and the deity's style. For instance, the deities in ISKCON Bengaluru include a *murti* of Vishnu as "Balaji," whose

---

15   See Loos 1998 (1908) for a now discredited evolutionary argument against ornament.
16   See Lyons 2004 for a study of the region's art of making *pichwai*, or devotional hangings, for the worship of Krishna deities.
17   See Packert 2010 for a detailed description of ornamentation as service in the Vrindavan temples.
18   See Hacker 2004 for how the status of people serving in the Jagannath, Puri, temple is related to the use of cloth.

original form is worshipped at the Sri Venkateswara temple in Tirupati, Andhra Pradesh. The Radha-Krishna deities in Bengaluru are dressed in a style different from those in the North, signaling a regional identity. The deities are usually dressed in typical South Indian "temple jewelry" and woven silks, while Radha is dressed in a manner that simulates the drape of a sari rather than the *gaghra-choli-odhani* (skirt and blouse with veil) found in Mayapur. Also, the deity figures themselves are made of metal in the style of South Indian temple bronzes and thus are distinctive from the marble deities found in other parts of India. Such semiotic and material links in the dress and adornment of the deities are influenced by the fact that geographical proximity and tradition matter in the experience of deity efficacy; that is, devotees who live in Bengaluru might regard the Vishnu deity at Tirupati as more powerful and may opt to worship at the ISKCON temple for convenience.[19] Thus the deities at ISKCON temples may be regarded as manifestations of other older forms with relationships reinforced through altar style and worship. In another example, a relationship exists between the Shrinathji temple in Nathdwara, Rajasthan, and the ISKCON Chowpatty temple in Mumbai, where images of Shrinathji, a child form of Krishna, are worshipped as royalty with offerings of food and clothing. (The temple in Nathdwara is referred to as a *haveli*, or mansion, being considered the home of the deity.) The Chowpatty temple includes a *murti* of Shrinathji in its main altar and also displays images of the deity in various costumes. In Mayapur, West Bengal, the stylistic proximity to Puri and Vrindavan is apparent with Jagannath deities installed and worshipped in a temple nearby and the area's Radha-Krishna and Gaur-Nitai (Chaitanya and his brother) deities dressed in a more ornate Vrindavan style rather than in simple cotton saris and *dhotis*.

Despite regional differences there is an identifiable ISKCON style of dressing the deities. The documented tradition of paintings by ISKCON artists and the compilation of deity *darshan* images, such as *Darsana* (Das 2005), have strongly influenced the idea of what an ISKCON deity should look like. ISKCON's style is perhaps best represented by the deity wardrobes in Mayapur, where the Radha-Madhava and Panchatattva deities have about 150 and 50 outfits, respectively, across multiple rooms in the temple. The garments as well as the rooms are considered sacred, and generally entry is restricted to priests and initiated devotees. Lakhs of rupees[20] are required for a complete set of festive garments for the Mayapur deities, and one or more donors sponsor these garments. Those who do not wish to fund a dress contribute by offering their

---

19   Personal communication with devotee at ISKCON Bengaluru temple, 2013.
20   At the time of writing, Rs100,000 was approximately equal to £1,200.

service and/or fabric yardage, supplies, and trims. Occasionally a devotee who runs a design firm or is skilled may make the clothing for the deities at no cost as their special offering to the deities. This is a big undertaking, because the deities are tall; the Radha-Madhava deities are about six feet tall, and the Panchatattva (Chaitanya and his associates) deities are about eight feet tall. The garments draw on ideas from various sources, and a walk through the deity wardrobe provides an overview of some of the inspirations, techniques, and materials.

The deity dresses in Mayapur range from the grandest Janmashtami clothes for Krishna's birthday to the simpler Radhashtami outfits for Radha's birthday. The Gaur Purnima dresses that celebrate Chaitanya's birth are situated in between these in terms of richness. Night-dresses are made of colorful woven fabrics and trims and are simpler than the ornate day-dresses that are embellished with embroidery and appliqué. Motifs on the garments are drawn mostly from nature. Some of the patterns are drawn from Indian motifs, such as the mango motifs, later associated in European textile history with paisley designs. Other garments are influenced by chinoiserie designs (Figure 2) and feature flowers, butterflies, and scrollwork rendered in an Orientalist style. Although the garments vary among themselves, they are consistent in one aspect. At any given *darshan*, all deities in the temple are dressed in outfits that are similar with the same fabric color, embroidery motifs, and accessories, although distinguished by gender and certain unique characteristics such as Krishna's iconic peacock feather. In this manner, an ISKCON style has developed both in India and abroad, and devotees have come to expect this even as they anticipate thematic changes according to the ritual calendar.

As an example of ISKCON style, let us consider the web archives of *murti darshans* at various temples in the United Kingdom and Ireland, including images of clothing that reference and combine ideas of stately European, Celtic, and Indian dress. In one such instance of fusion style, Krishna's costume is a cross-cultural celebration that bears stylistic similarity to both a *gherdar jama* (a Mughal-inspired costume featuring a sewn coat with full skirt) and a plaid kilt, while Radha's *lehenga-choli* (skirt and blouse) and *odhani* (veil or scarf) resemble a European woman's blouse, skirt, and shawl. In Figure 3 we see a day outfit for the Mayapur deities in India that is influenced both by European and Indian aesthetic preferences and cultural norms. Designed by a British devotee who has been associated with the movement since its beginning, the costume pays homage to her life and work in the United Kingdom and to her more recent service in India. The garment includes a red blouse, a gold skirt with a red bustle, and a hooded cape for modesty. Such styles continue to be inspiring for devotees, especially those who make garments for the deities installed in

FIGURE 2   Detail of embroidered Chinese peacock on a deity's skirt.
             MAYAPUR, 2012. IMAGE BY AUTHOR

their homes. In the screengrab from a global deity-dressing group on Facebook
(Figure 4), one can see how devotees continue to share sources of style inspiration drawn from European historical sources, resonating the devotee's cultural background or the temple's specific location in the West. The process of
cross-cultural borrowing and appropriation in Indian garments certainly did
not start with foreign devotees in ISKCON. Going back into colonial history, we
find Orientalist fusion in the production of British textiles through motifs such
as the paisley or wallpaper designs on saris (McGowan 2009: 105) and images of
Indian rulers dressed in British fashions (Codell 2011: 115, 136).

     With key people in the Gaudiya Math and ISKCON having lived during the
nineteenth and twentieth centuries an aesthetic of cultural borrowing would
not have been unknown, reinforced by such colonial buildings in Calcutta as
the Victoria Memorial. Indeed, the capital New Delhi was itself planned with
the form of an imperial Mughal *durbar* so that the Viceroy's Palace could over-
look the colonial bureaucracy, the princes of India, and, increasingly, events
such as state funerals and national holidays, when rulers and their entourage
had to be publicly visible (Cohn 1987: 72). The aesthetic of ornamentation as
power was enacted by the Raj through a mimetic monarchy in its colonies that
utilized concepts and practices such as *durbar* (Cannadine 2002). *Durbar* rituals acquired a heightened political importance in British India with the grand

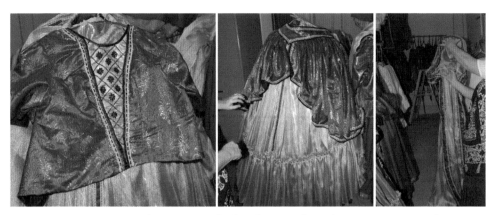

FIGURE 3   Day outfit for the deity Radha based on an eighteenth-century European style.
            MAYAPUR, 2012. IMAGE BY AUTHOR

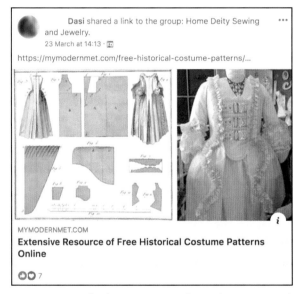

FIGURE 4   Facebook post on ISKCON home deity sewing and
            jewelry site, 2019.
            IMAGE BY AUTHOR

durbar for George V when he visited India in 1911, allowing British rule to distinguish itself as well as to create similarities with the native kings and princes.

In her analysis of the colonial Indian court of Pudukkotai in South India, Waghorne (1994) develops the notion of the *durbar* as a cultural space that was shared with the British. She argues that when *durbar* rituals gained ascendency over temple rituals in this principality, a more primordial, non-orthodox conception of divine kingship came to the fore and acquired a material and spiritual locus in ornament such as the king's clothing and paraphernalia. A similar commingling of Indian and British elements would have been pervasive in daily life in colonial India. In the nineteenth century prints of British royalty, for instance, would have hung on the walls of shops alongside traditional prints of the deities Krishna and Kali (Kipling 1891: 340). Against this history of colonial mixing, the temple's congregational space could be considered as performing the same role as the traditional king's *durbar*, or meeting room, with an emphasis on attractive deity garments. Although heightened by the presence of foreign devotees, stylistic appropriation would not have been unknown to the ISKCON founder Prabhupada even while he was in India, and this approach is reflected in the style of the monumental temple (Temple of the Vedic Planetarium, or TOVP) being built currently in Mayapur (Figure 5).

FIGURE 5   Signboard with computer rendering of the TOVP.
MAYAPUR, 2012. IMAGE BY AUTHOR

Indian historical and mythological texts, contemporary travelers' accounts, colonial accounts, and paintings show that gold and silver textiles were associated with royalty, prosperity, and power. One of the key elements of a *durbar* was the importance of opulent and appropriate dress as worn by native rulers, since this added to the prestige of the Raj as well as signaling the rulers' willingness to be representatives of Empire. Historically, embellishment was integral to Mughal, Hindu, and British monarchy with the craft of *zardozi* embroidery arriving in India under the patronage of Islamic rulers of the Delhi Sultanate (1206–1526 CE) and flourishing till the end of the Mughal empire (1526–1857 CE). The craft was adopted by other Hindu and Muslim rulers who set up embroidery centers in Gujarat, Rajasthan, and Bengal. After British rule *zardozi* was incorporated into the colonial textile trade but maintained its regal associations. For instance, the *zardozi* embroidery on the coronation gown of Queen Alexandra (1844–1925 CE, wife of King Edward VII, 1841–1910 CE) attracted nineteenth-century aristocratic women and their sense of sartorial drama with its glitter and maximum visibility (Strasdin 2012: 160).

ISKCON's deity embellishment techniques thus indirectly draw on the historic aspects of *zardozi*, relating connotations of "power dressing" by Indian and British royalty to the *darshans* of contemporary Hindu deities. The purpose of dazzling garments in most temples is to overwhelm and enchant the spectator (see Gell in Mohan 2017a: 225). Twinkling sequins and beads, and shiny silk and sateen fabrics, help to make the *murtis* seem luminous and alive. Devotees use evocative terms, such as "opulent" and "effulgent," in association with the physical properties of the deity garments in Mayapur as well as the deity's qualities of absolute intelligence, perfection, and beauty. Further, an etymological connection to notions of prosperity (and auspiciousness) can be found in the very material of embroidery when Indian artisans attach shiny metal discs or sequins to create luminescent surfaces: the word "sequin" is related to the Arabic *sikkah*, a minting die, and the Italian *zecchino*, an Italian coin. *Zardozi* embroidery continues to be a popular embellishment technique in Hindu temples with competition among the various sects to stage daily *darshans* of attractively dressed *murtis*. Numerous embroidery workshops produce deity clothing in Vrindavan, and ornate clothing is especially popular with the Swaminarayan sect as well as wealthy Hindu industrialists, such as the Birla family, who fund temples in various parts of India.[21]

---

21   Today, *zardozi* has a broad clientele throughout India and the world, and embroidered garments have been popularized by Bollywood films and Indian/global fashion designers. The technique is used on clothing, footwear, home furnishings, and the like, and international firms use embroidery ateliers in India to execute commissions for clients.

6   Embroidery as Devotional Practice

Religious practices can be regarded as traditional actions with effects pertaining to the (experience of the) sacred. The work done by objects, aesthetics, and senses in a religious context may be studied through the observation of techniques, which have been defined as "efficacious actions upon matter" (Lemonnier 1992: 4, following Leroi-Gourhan 1993 [1964]) and "an action which is effective and traditional" (Mauss 2006 [1935]: 82). While "technique" simply refers to a certain manner of doing things, the issue is complicated in the context of religion, where a technique is considered to have otherworldly, magical effects by acting on an invisible, divine entity or sacred force. The concept of religious efficacy in this context is also one that is a fraught subject for empirical study as the devotee performs actions whose accomplishment draws on the original ontological efficacy of God as the being that has no cause outside itself. The discussion of religious techniques, hence, involves the culture's own conception of efficacy[22] as well as *how* a researcher might go about studying such efficacy by observing ways of making and doing (Naji and Douny 2009). Using this idea, the following paragraphs focus on a small group of people in the Mayapur community (thirty international devotees and twenty Bengali embroiderers and tailors, devotees and nondevotees) who work only for the temple and make clothing for the deities.

A new festival dress for all the deities takes about three months to complete. Local Bengali men in their early 20s to late 30s embroider the fabric. Out of the twenty-odd workers, eight to ten travel from Swarupganj, a town across the river, and the remaining live within Mayapur. Most were born and raised in West Bengal; some are immigrants from Bangladesh. All are Hindus, and many are initiated ISKCON devotees. The workers have acquired their knowledge and skills from working in Kolkata and Vrindavan or have been trained in Mayapur. It took about six months to become proficient with the *ari* needle, with trainees first learning the necessary hand-wrist motion with a sewing needle, an *ari* hook, or a matchstick. Once the trainee had gained the habit (Hindi, *adath*) of using the *ari* he was then given a task.

The embroidery that is done with a regular sewing needle is *zardozi*, which takes its name from *zar*, a Persian word for gold. Work done with a hooked *ari* needle is called *zari*. A combination of both techniques is often used in the same object. *Zardozi* is heavier and more ornamental than *zari* and requires thicker base fabrics, such as velvet. *Zari*, however, is executed on lighter fabrics, such as silk and satin. Deity garments generally combine the two techniques

---

22   The word efficacy is related to the Latin term *efficere* ("to accomplish").

with a dominance of *zari* work since the technique is faster. The replacement of *zardozi* with *zari* means that the task is completed much faster. The visual effect is similar, but one also runs the risk of the embroidery unraveling easily, and so the choice to use one or the other is a pragmatic one. The *ari* stitch is a simple chain stitch that is executed with tambour hook needles of varying thicknesses on a fabric with a prestamped design. In Mayapur a senior devotee conceives and draws the original embroidery pattern on a thick tracing paper and, once it is approved by the head priest, holes are pricked along the lines of the design on the tracing paper using a pricking needle. The paper is then positioned on the stretched fabric, and a paste of zinc oxide and paraffin oil is smeared over the design using a rag. This is the stamping (*chap*) process where the color is transferred through the needle pricks onto the fabric, and the tracing paper is removed to reveal the faint outlines of the pattern on the cloth. A contrasting colored paste is used such that a blue tinted paste may be used on lighter fabrics and a white nontinted paste is used on darker fabrics. A sample of the embroidery is first created and showed to the head priest of the temple. After he approves it, the pattern is scaled to the dimensions of the various deities, pricked, and then transferred onto large prestretched pieces of cloth on frames. The frame on which the cloth is stretched can accommodate fabrics of up to 10 feet wide and 10 feet long and can be adjusted for smaller dimensions. Multiple small items or single large items can be embroidered on a single frame.

Different thicknesses of needles (*ari, chunch, sui*) are used to embroider the design depending on whether they are to be used in conjunction with a single strand or two strands of thread. The threads (*daga*) are made either of cotton or silk/synthetic gold (*kasab*), to attach sequins (*sitra*) or beads (*chir, katdana*). The tambour hook needles are made of iron and resemble the shape of a fine crochet needle with cotton threads that are tightly wrapped around the shafts so that they can be held comfortably. When the needle tips become dull and cannot hook the thread easily a sharp file or blade (*korad*) is used to facet the notch. (A large-eyed sewing needle is used for a process called "loading" that is explained later in this section.) Sequins are called *chamki*, a word that refers to their quality of *chamak*, or shine. Another name for sequins in Bengali and Hindi is *sitara* ("star"). Sequins are manufactured in plastic in addition to the traditional metal, which allows for new visual effects. Styles of sequins, such as "disco" and *barsathi* ("rainy"), derive their names from their ability to reflect and refract light in different ways. The *barsathi*, or rain-sequin, is so called because each sequin when viewed under the light appears to ripple and move like water. This apparent motion brings to mind the expressive use of ideophones in everyday language. A devotee in Chennai, for instance, referred to the kind of glittering fabric that she bought for the deity as *pala*; the word *pala* is a colloquial term for "shimmer" in Tamil. While using this term she also gestured with her hands and shook her palms as if to physically express the motion that accompanies the visual experience of shimmer.

Workers sit cross-legged on the floor on reed mats in summer and cushions in winter. The wooden frames are raised to the level of their armpits so that they can comfortably rest their arms on the frames while working (Figure 6). Each worker has a small thick cloth that either is used to station their toolbox, beads, and sequins or is placed under their right arm so that the fabric is not soiled and briskly moving needles do not accidentally snag the embroidery. The proper posture involves placing the left hand under the stretched fabric and the right hand over the fabric. The needle is wielded by the right hand in an up-down-and-twist motion while the left hand catches the thread and winds it around the hooked tip of the *ari* needle when it is below the fabric surface (Figure 7). The execution of a stitch involves mind-hand-eye and other forms of sensory coordination, such as attention to the sounds produced.

FIGURE 6   Embroidering a *Janmashtami* dress.
MAYAPUR, 2012. IMAGE BY AUTHOR

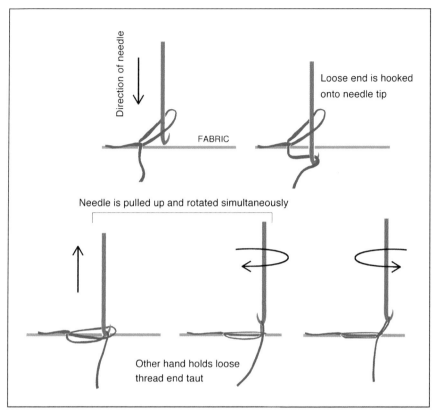

FIGURE 7   Steps of making a chain stitch on a taut fabric using the *ari* needle. From left to
right, top to bottom.
IMAGE BY AUTHOR

Three different sounds are made by one *ari* stitch, and an experienced embroiderer uses these sounds as a guide, to lessen the strain on his eyes. One
sound is the dull tapping sound of the needle's curved tip entering the fabric
from above. This is followed by a split-second pause while the left hand under
the fabric winds the thread around the needle tip, and then the "plop" of the
needle being pulled out of the fabric is accompanied by the softer squeak of
the silk fabric as the needle passes out.

The *ari* stitch is used in combinations with beads, sequins, and appliqué
to embellish the surface of the fabric. There are many micro-motions that go
into making a simple border of sequins and beads, from ensuring that they
are correctly positioned to reinforcing the stitches and maintaining the necessary tautness. Part of the skill lies in maintaining consistency and a regular pace while finding new ways to maximize the reflective effects of shiny

materials. Many small details, such as different planes of light, and different shapes and material can be manipulated to add visual interest and enhance the garment. The workers emphasized the importance of quality when the embroidery has to be both long-lasting and attractive. For example, the seemingly straightforward execution of pearl beads (*mothi*) in a circular pattern around the central flower motif (Figure 8) can be done in different ways depending on how tightly one wants the beads to be reinforced. The fish-scale pattern of the central flower petals is visually arresting but one of the more time-consuming techniques.

Loading is another technique that heightens the visual effect of the design. It refers to the process by which height and thickness are added to an embroidered section by padding it first with thick cotton thread or strips of cloth (Figure 9). The preferred method when using a sewing needle to create *zardozi* embroidery involves sewing over the loaded area with thick cotton thread in a satin stitch, reinforcing it with a grid of thin cotton thread and then embroidering over it with a silk thread or precut pieces of metal spring (*bulen*). Another method that is used when a high degree of padding is required involves creating pre-embroidered pieces (leaves, petals, and so on) that are partly sewn onto the fabric with an *ari* and then stuffed with thin strips of cotton fabric, as one would fill a stuffed toy. Either one or both of these methods can be used to make three-dimensional forms on the fabric that create visual interest.

Embroidery techniques use manual labor, and workers have to be highly skilled as well as physically strong. They must be capable of repetitive actions over long periods of time, often in stressful positions. Yet, as one worker pointed out, embroidery is also the work of the mind (hindi, *dimag ka kam*); one has to think and guide the actions of the hand even when such gestures

FIGURE 8   Belt for deity dress.
MAYAPUR, 2013. IMAGE BY AUTHOR

FIGURE 9   Embroidering with needle and silk thread over a previously loaded area. Video
            still.
            MAYAPUR, 2013. IMAGE BY AUTHOR

are mastered and have become routine. Also, decisions are constantly being
made about *how* to do things—that is, which tools and supplies to use, what
techniques to use, and how much time and energy to invest in a particular
task. Even for skilled embroiderers these decisions were avenues to a devotional consciousness. Workers constantly made decisions about the qualities
and values of the garment through the application of technical virtuosity; they
used this virtuosity as a means of differentiating their attitude toward work for
the deities and work for a secular purpose. Nondevotional work was implied
to be routine or ordinary, whereas deity work was by implication something
extraordinary or special. The former could be done by anybody with a little
training, but the latter demanded a higher level of skill and knowledge, limited
to a select group. It also required a concern for the qualities of the completed
product. The refinement, or what the workers called in English the "finishing,"
of the embroidery directly affected their identity and reputation, especially
when they were already initiates.[23] Those who were devotees and/or initiates
derived satisfaction from knowing that what they did was a "direct service" for
the deities (a term that implied great soteriological value) and believed that
when they died they would ascend to the heavens and continue to make clothing for Radha and Krishna.

---

23   Personal communication with Mayapur embroidery workers, 2012–2013.

7   Values in the Classroom and Beyond

Deity garments enchant in a couple of different ways. As stated earlier, enchantment (Gell 1992) is a process by which human and artefactual agency are enmeshed in a network of intentionalities. Acts of making and doing things around the deity help devotees to develop relationships with each other and with the deity, with the belief that the latter possesses a mind as well as intentionality. We have seen how luminous garments and the decoration of the temple altar helped to create an atmosphere of auspiciousness and an aura of power around the deities. One particularly articulate devotee who had been in ISKCON from its early days in the West spoke of a "paradigm shift" that turned doing into devotion by engaging devotees' every aspect until they were actually doing what Krishna wanted them to do. Spiritual growth meant evolving from thinking about what they wanted to do to what Krishna would want them to do. In this sense, one could say they had been subjectivated as Krishna devotees.

Krishna is a deity who is personified in a highly human manner (as baby, child, youth, king),—strengthened by his love for his devotees as well as in need of protection, depending on the form in which he is worshipped. For example, a baby Krishna *murti* would elicit feelings of maternal nurturing. His protection includes adornment and amulets, as well as other modes, such as how the congregation can view him—for instance, via mini-*darshans* or glimpses called *jhankis*. In the famous Banke Bihari temple in Vrindavan, priests are afraid that their beloved Krishna will be seduced by the loving gazes of his devotees and will run away with them; so in this temple the altar curtain is closed every few minutes during *darshan* in order to break the power of the congregational gaze. In the Nathdwara temple in Rajasthan, Shrinathji, a child form of Krishna, is worshipped in *jhankis*. These short-duration *jhankis* protect Shrinathji, who is considered to be vulnerable to the evil eye (Hindi/Urdu: *nazar*; Sanskrit: *drishti*). Simultaneously, the concept of *jhankis* in this context can be enhanced by considering these experiences not simply as glimpses that emphasize the short duration but as "tableau vivants" (Lyons 2004: 20) that draw the spectator into the mood (*bhava*) of the deity as presented on that day.

To understand the phenomenon of *darshan* as (desire for) immersive devotional experience that is oriented toward the deity figure, we can perhaps turn to Gell (1998: 81) and his analysis of the decorated object as "never fully possessed at all but ... always in the process of becoming possessed." He states, in the context of complex patterns, that to endure over time social relationships have to be founded on unfinished business. "The essence of exchange, as a binding force, is the delay, or lag, between transactions which, if the exchange relation is to endure, should never result in perfect reciprocation, but always in some renewed, residual, imbalance" (ibid.). Similarly, *darshan* could be regarded as an interocular exchange that is never completely reciprocatory or satisfactory for the devotee because of the power imbalance between deity and devotee. Indeed, devotees may perceive it as a momentary but real physical experience, especially in those temples where the congregation ques up in single file to see the deity. Although devotees might speak of their *darshanic* experiences in glowing terms, the "dissatisfaction" of a *darshanic* experience, if one can so term it, is a result of the unfinished business of devotional desire that is necessary and contributes to ritual efficacy as a repetition of the process. The hierarchy between deity and devotee that gives rise to this imbalance and supplicatory desire is not a given but has to be sustained by forms of external and internal agency. The deity garments' aesthetics work apotropaically on a cognitive and phenomenological level so that they attract as well as overwhelm the viewer's perception. This process in turn accompanies or induces emotions of awe, mystification, and even fear that make the deity seem more potent and efficacious.

The Mayapur sewing room contributes to the creation of moods (*bhavas*) and the *darshanic* effect by acting as a space where people get together to painstakingly embroider and sew garments for the deities. In the process many of them, as previously mentioned, perceive their labor not simply as a job but as devotional service in response to a higher calling. In fact, although there are paid employees, many of the devotees who visit the temple simply offer their services (*sewa*) for free as a form of devotional practice. Further, while clothing can be a spontaneous devotional offering from lay devotees, it is more often carefully designed to project the power and image of the deity, create a mood of reverence, and act as a preaching tool to attract new devotees. Thus Mayapur *darshans* and their images are devices that both attract pilgrims to the temple and ensure that the deity is perceived as powerful and agentive. Along with lay devotees and the sewing room's employees, the priests who dress the deities on the altar are also actively engaged in this process.

To understand how devotees are trained to qualify as priests on the temple's altar as well as for worship at home, one should explore how priests are trained formally at the Mayapur Academy, an educational institute on the ISKCON campus in Mayapur.[24] The deity-dressing course at the Academy is part of a larger deity-worship program and lasts for about two weeks (Figure 10). It is offered in two languages, Bengali and English, with students from India and the rest of the world. During this time, students learn the many details involved

---

24   This topic was also covered in Mohan 2015.

in presenting the deities as opulent as well as approachable. While much of the richness of the garments is in their color and embroidery, the instructors teach the students how to enhance these qualities using jewelry and drapery. Students are provided with large figures of Krishna and Radha or Gaur and Nitai (Chaitanya and his brother) as well as busts to practice on. Krishna's dancing *tribhanga* (three bends) form is animated through flowing fabrics, flower garlands, and bead necklaces. The asymmetrical style of Krishna's posture, turban, and dress is deemed to complement the symmetrical modesty of his consort Radha's posture and garments.

During one session the instructor informed the class that Krishna's dress had to be confident and bold, whereas Radha had to be dressed to seem sweet as well as approachable, in keeping with her role as the mediator between devotees and Krishna. The clothing and altar decoration was also to be oriented toward enhancing the frontality of the deities' forms and, in particular, the mood on the faces of the deities. Although access to instruction in the training of priests and devotees is taken for granted today, previously, formal training was not the norm. Instead, this approach to training arose with the felt need to create regularity across the many temples and their standard of deity worship. The European instructor who taught this deity-dressing module had joined ISKCON in the early 1980s, when he met a devotee selling books, and, frustrated with his job, he decided to visit India. The ISKCON center in Delhi was in a house at that time, and the devotees put him up in a warehouse next to the kitchen. When the cook left, he was tasked with the job and slowly moved on to working on priestly duties. In the matter of a few years he had moved to Mayapur, where he served as a priest, and in the early 2000s he started teaching the deity-dressing courses in Mayapur. Part of this phenomenon was the concern that ISKCON altars had a certain level of worship to maintain and that with the global expansion of the organization such standardization of quality was necessary.

One way of creating feelings of intimacy as well as distance with the deity was through draping and wrapping techniques. The module emphasized an appropriate distance between priest and deity and in doing so seemed to partly anticipate the protective or defensive function of apotropaic ornamental techniques such as luminosity, discussed earlier. The instructor's repeated emphasis on doing what was appropriate also arose from his training within ISKCON, where the founder Prabhupada clearly demarcated boundaries between the community and a Bengali Vaishnav sect called the *sahajiyas*. *Sahaja* means "easy" or "natural" in Sanskrit, and *sahajiyas* are perceived in Bengal as a lower-caste, abject group. They are also considered to be apostates because of *tantric* worship that involves sex and ingestion of bodily fluids. Part of

FIGURE 10   Student practices dressing mannequins of deities. Note the busts and figures in
the background.
MAYAPUR, 2012. IMAGE BY AUTHOR

ISKCON's disgust with the group stems from what they consider to be distasteful practices and their excessive intimacy with the deity as well as the group's own origin as a middle-class, rationalizing force in the nineteenth century. Further, *sahajīya* practices were/are considered fake by ISKCON since they are believed to achieve nothing. By contrast, ISKCON's practices were regarded as efficacious, and this effectiveness lay partly in knowing one's boundaries. Thus the boundaries that were reinforced were not just between devotee and deity and were certainly not limited to the altar; they were ultimately intended to remind the devotee of the efficacy of ISKCON's worship practices and to demarcate the entity from other groups.

While emphasizing the intimacy of the gaze in *darshan*, the instructor added that opulent dressing was needed both for Krishna's pleasure and to ensure that devotees maintained an appropriate respectful relationship with the deity. The students were told anecdotes of events at other temples that proved that Krishna could take the form of anything, including stone, and so they were to approach the deity forms with respect, because they were not material but sentient divinity. Students were urged to remember that Krishna had senses and that while dressing the classroom mannequins they must treat them like *murtis* and not poke pins into the figures in their haste and carelessness. The instructor had also developed an exercise called P(A)IN whereby students learned to use their capacity for sensory empathy as a device to attribute a mind, sentience, and subjecthood to the deity. This learning was subsequently reinforced through the process of examination: students dressed the deities and were evaluated and sent away with grades and printed diplomas. When asked later what the most important thing was that they learned, they said it was that Krishna was a person and that the *murti* could not be treated casually. Part of graduating successfully from such deity-worship programs was to reassure the instructors that certain values would be carried through into worship whether in the temple or home. Many devotees practiced home deity worship, and their ideas indicated how materials and aesthetics could be used in a manner that was part of a wider cosmology. Those devotees who made deity clothing (either for other devotees or for temples) or who practiced deity worship on a regular basis seemed to filter their ideas and concerns through their particular *sewa*. Some devotees believed that the attachments of material life were temporary and that materials were ultimately worthless but that while they lived these materials also served as the medium through which they communicated and related with Krishna.

Krishna Consciousness is based on an antimaterialist philosophy wherein pessimism about material existence is a criterion for spiritual development (Goswami 2012: 100). A Krishna-conscious society and self are considered to be alternatives to the "false truths, false happiness, and false consciousness" provided by Western materialism (Vande Berg and Kniss 2008: 83). Antimaterialism could take the form of monastic withdrawal and rejection of the material world, but for most devotees it is part of daily attempts to keep Krishna at the center of one's life even while residing in the material world. While considering the world as theophany, householder devotees negotiate the values of the outside world by using objects, bodies, and senses in a manner oriented toward Krishna and therefore spiritualized. So-called transcendental values could thus be sustained by the heightened sensuality and materiality of deity-worship practices.

The work of differentiating the spiritual from the material was evinced in the way devotees thought of themselves and others. The term *karmi* commonly refers to nondevotees or materialists trapped in the worldly cycle of actions (*karma*) and reactions. Since their actions are channeled toward Krishna, devotees believe that they would be freed from karmic consequences and the eternal cycle of birth and reincarnation (*samsara*). Materials were also part of this categorization of worlds, and these values entered the workspace (sewing room, classroom) as ideas about the production of garments. Invoking the Vaishnav philosophical and ontological concept of *gunas*, or modes of material nature, one devotee described the human problem as one of being good at making and destroying things but very bad at looking after things and sustaining them. Although she did not explicitly use these words, her description evoked the three categories of *rajas* (passion), *sattva* (harmony), and *tamas* (destruction). She applied this logic to the case of the deity garments, lamenting the fact that the poor storage and the humidity in Mayapur easily damaged the silk outfits and tarnished the embellishment. Others mentioned the problem of working with "*karmi* materials," a term they used for shoddily made trims and fabrics that evoked a larger ethos of deterioration or loss of quality. Frequently devotees took trips to Kolkata to buy supplies and would comment on the problem of ostentatiousness in Indian clothing in general when they encountered garments that looked gorgeous but were not made to last. The current opulence of plastic, sequins, and glass was contrasted to earlier decades when one could buy a sari with real silver or gold brocade, extractable at the end of the garment's life and therefore a more sustainable form of wealth. All these anecdotes echoed concerns about value and how it changed easily in the age of *kali*—everything has to be instant and as ostentatious as possible.

Kali yuga is the present age in cyclical Hindu cosmology and represents the maximum decline of morality, order, and wisdom in the world. The four *yugas* or epochs in the macrocosmic Hindu theory of time and society are *krita, treta, dwapar*, and *kali*. The *yugas* move in a cycle of repetition and progressive degeneration with the current age of *kali* representing the most chaos and loss of coherence before the beginning of a new cosmic cycle. Durations of the *yugas* vary depending on the source, but what is common is the progressive sense of degeneration and chaos from the *krita* to the *kali yuga*. The common Hindu belief is that progressive degeneration occurs through the ages culminating in *kali yuga*, when most people are born as untouchables, or *shudras*. Within ISKCON's specific views on karma and *kali yuga* it is only through reformatory practices and cultivation of knowledge that one can become a Brahmin.[25] The initiated foreign devotees mentioned in this monograph regarded themselves as Brahmins within a revitalized caste system. Devotees' descriptions of *kali* seemed to equate the age with materialism as a superficial mode of life whereby the real had been replaced by the illusion of the fake. Garment

---

25   "*Janmana jayate sudrah, samskarad bhaved dvijah, veda-pathad bhaved vipra, brahma janatiti brahmanah.*" This Sanskrit sentence is often quoted as *shastra*, or scripture, in ISKCON to support conversion of foreigners. It deemphasizes the importance of birth and reinforces the importance of reformation and initiation into Brahmin status. Prabhupada explains this as: "By birth one is a *sudra*, by the purificatory process one becomes a *dvija*, by study of the Vedas one becomes a *vipra*, and one who knows Brahman is a *brahmana*." *Srimad Bhagavatam*, 3:11:26, Purport by Prabhupada.

makers discussed this by contrasting illusory ostentation with real opulence as in that of the deities. The mood of opulence was associated with fabrics that held intrinsic value, such as the Benares silk sari, whereas ostentation was associated with garments that were garish and shoddy and whose value did not outlast their purchase. Here, objects and humans were being subjected to the same kind of analytical perspective, and one entity was used to critique and understand the other.

8 Circulation of Images and Imagery

So far we have discussed the importance of visuality in the temple's *darshan* and how seeing becomes a form of apprehending the truth of divinity through transformative experiences. While this theme forms the core of my exploration, we also must consider the lifecycle of cloth objects—their flow and relocation through images and representations. In this section we examine what happens both literally and figuratively when deity images circulate. How is their performativity translated, and what kind of values do they afford in new domains? Objects used in Hindu worship include deity images as well as the paraphernalia used to worship them. In addition, in contemporary temples the impact of *darshan* resonates through other media (calendars, posters, stickers, photos, computers, electronic devices) and images printed on various objects (magnets, badges, T-shirts, and prayer bead bags). These may protect against misfortune, be tools for meditation, and act as means for liberation from rebirth. The fact that they work across the various senses does not make them any less material in South Asian traditions (Jacobsen, Aktor, and Myrvold, eds. 2015: 3), where forms of matter, substances, and bodily perceptions are capable of morphing into, and affecting, one another.

The power of the gaze in India is documented as being both potentially benevolent and malevolent, and as attractive as well as repellent (Babb 1981; Bhatti and Pinney 2011). In his study of the ritual art of Indian chromolithographs of deity images, Pinney (2004) argues for the importance of aesthetics in enabling two-dimensional images to serve as a conduit between beholder and deity. Drawing on Buck-Morss's (1992) observation that modern aesthetics is anesthetics, Pinney (2004: 18–19) challenges the modern science of aesthetics as detached contemplation, predicated on a Kantian distance (Kant 2007 [1790]) or absence of the body, and proposes a return to the discourse of the body through corporeal aesthetics, or "corpothetics," and an emphasis on perception by feeling. Morgan (1998: 26–27) further argues that the concept of aesthetics as a Kantian disinterestedness is of limited use in studying the visuality and materiality of worship and its modalities. He notes that the disinterested and detached judgment of the aesthetic pertains to the "representation of something taken up into the imagination, and understanding, not to the object itself" (ibid.: 26). Emphasizing the erotic aspects of vision in Hindu devotion (*bhakti*) in the Pushtimargi sect based in Western India, Jain (2007: 260) highlights the "sensualised libidinal involvement with the icon" during the visual engagement of *darshan*. She further contrasts the visual experience and desire of *darshan* to post-Enlightenment aesthetics "predicated on an autonomous subject that has self-critically distanced itself from its sensory passions, desires, and affects, even as sensual apprehension is acknowledged as their basis" (ibid.). As Davis (1997: 50) cautions, although Indian audiences look at their deity images attentively the goal is not just visual experience: "They valued a personal, emotional relationship with the deity mediated through the divine presence in the icon." The translucence of the icon invoked in the design and iconography of the image (*murti*) acts as a means for the devotee to apprehend the deity's totality. In these contexts sight is integral to the process of devotion as insight (*darshan*), and the importance of the power of sight is embedded into the very making and reception of the deity image. For example, the ritual "awakening" of the completed deity image in Hindu tradition is accomplished by a special ceremony in which the priest opens the deity's eyes (*netronmilana*).

In his study of the complex afterlife of colonial (and postcolonial) mimesis in art, Pinney (2004: 220) states that local Indian artists from Nathdwara, Rajasthan, were invited to the ISKCON offices in New York to train their new illustrators. These illustrators were ethnically non-Indian but were considered heirs to the tradition of Indian artists such as B. G. Sharma (Pinney 2004: 147; Sharma 2004; Tripurari and Sharma 2005) and adept at making devotional paintings. Devotional posters have been popular for decades with colonial Bengali chromolithographs of Chaitanya, for instance, depicting the saint dancing in ecstasy during *sankirtan* (congregational dancing and singing). But the invitation of Nathdwara artists happened at a time when ISKCON was in its infancy, and there was a tremendous push to translate, transcribe, and illustrate books ranging from scripture to treatises by Prabhupada. Through each of these phases substyles of ISKCON art developed that either drew more directly from Indian devotional and classical painting styles or combined Indian influences with European naturalism, Japanese animation/anime, and so on. Describing the saturated images of pale-skinned individuals used as ISKCON book illustrations, Jain (2007: 202–203) states that these illustrations of events from Krishna's life are located within a textual arena and do not need to serve as devotional icons. They can take on aspects of realism (albeit slanted to-ward Western perceptions) that other Indian artists reject in favor of effica-cious frontality, that is, the manner in which the frontal image of a deity is represented in *darshanic* images. Yet the sacralization of ISKCON's publication of the *Bhagavad Gita* (Prabhupada 1986) also allows for such unconventional imagery to be re-incorporated into *darshan*. For example, a home altar that I saw in Chennai featured a Tamil translation of the *Gita* with an image of the Goswami saints and a *murti* of the child Krishna. The cover image of the *Gita* depicted Krishna as Arjuna's charioteer during the war of the Mahabharata, and the book itself was displayed frontally, much like a Hindu icon. Although such an image by itself may be valued but not be worshipped, its situation on the cover of the *Gita* indicated an ISKCON modality of worship (book as icon) as well as how images and objects interacted in ritual practices.

The sensorial and affective value and style of images (what might be called their corpothetic excess) could either strengthen or dilute the Krishna-centered emphasis of ISKCON. Krishna-Kali prints sold in the town of Nabadwip, bor-dering Mayapur, feature Krishna seated next to an unusually docile Goddess Kali, enraptured by his flute-playing (Figure 11, lower left). This print is clearly not intended for a staunch ISKCON devotee, who would be uncomfortable with the association of Vaishnavs with Shaktas (worshippers of *Shakti* or the primordial female force). However, the fact that such an image is circulated so close to Mayapur indicates that it is necessary in a state where Durga/Kali *puja* is the most important festival; it also caters to those devotees for whom such associations are welcome. For example, a Bengali ISKCON preacher vis-ited the village of Jirat around the time of Durga *puja/pujo* and was invited by the people of the town to view their *pandal* (pavilion) as well as give a talk. The preacher's discourse did not ignore or repudiate the deities Kali and Shiva but repositioned them as Krishna's "prime devotees" and thus made them subordi-nates whose devotion was to be emulated by humans. Similarly, a viewer could interpret Kali's role in the Krishna-Kali print as one of subordination that re-inforced Krishna's power rather than threaten ISKCON's ideological purity. In brief, such an image could serve as a soft preaching device outside the confines of the ISKCON campus. In other parts of India and the world the symbolic flexibility and multivalency of images that we have seen at a regional level in Bengal (both in image and discourse) may be replaced by something else. The presence or absence of certain images, and the ways in which they relate to scripture and practice, indicates what ISKCON wishes to (de)emphasize and could be considered an extension of the "semiotic ideology" (Keane 2003) that shapes the devotional subject.

FIGURE 11   Posters from Nabadwip featuring the Mayapur deities as well as Krishna and Kali
            on lower left side.
            MAYAPUR, 2013. IMAGE BY AUTHOR

The "inter-ocularity" (Pinney 2004: 34) and ubiquity of art forms such as draping, painting, chromolithography, sculpture, photography, and several others, facilitate visual inter-referencing between different registers of "secular"
and "religious," invoking devotional connotations in nondevotional contexts.
Examples of material inter-referencing across religious and national boundaries can be found in the clothing of *murtis* in other Hindu groups in the West.
For instance, the Bochasanwasi Shri Akshar Purushottam Swaminarayan
Sanstha (BAPS) is a major group within the Swaminarayan sect of Hinduism
whose U.K. headquarters are in Neasden, London. A photo from the Shri temple's gift shop shows the deities Shiva and Parvati against the backdrop of the
Indian flag. Seemingly influenced by ISKCON's emphasis on *mise-en-scène*, the
aesthetics of the Indian flag backdrop in the BAPS shrine was translated into
the color, texture, and drape of the deities' costumes, including Parvati's mul-
tipleated and lustrous tricolor sari. The goddess's sari is draped in the Gujarati
style, communicating a distinct regional Indian identity to visitors and the pre-
dominantly Gujarati worshippers of the sect. In the case of ISKCON centers
that are abroad there is a lack of a sole (Bengali) regional identity, and individual temples may try to infuse a local flavor. For instance, altars of temples
in the United Kingdom may feature the deities dressed in garments whose

colors and motifs draw on local traditions such as the plaid fabrics used for kilts, three-leaf clovers, and Celtic knots. Simultaneously, when new designs for garments are received negatively, the subsequent debates and negotiations help to shed light on the values of deity dressing and worship in the group.

As an example of this material negotiation, there is the instance when the aesthetics of the Mayapur altar (regarded as exemplary in setting the standard for other temples) became a point of debate through the global circulation of images. In 2007 a group of Chinese devotees undertook a pilgrimage to Mayapur, bringing with them offerings of silk fabric for the deities. The devotees also brought along with them stories of hardship in practicing their faith openly. The Chinese devotees were eager to do something for the deities, and, in turn, the Mayapur head priest and designer wanted to reciprocate, because the pilgrims were sustaining their devotion under adversity. The garment designer saw this as an opportunity to make something that would attract devotees in East Asia as well as signaling the temple's support of its global branches. She designed a wraparound garment that would serve as a night-dress; it was a fusion of Chinese and Japanese styles and was labeled a "kimono." (This reference was considered respectful since it also drew on the connotations of the *gopis* as cultivated handmaidens to the deities.) The Chinese devotees made the night-dresses using the floral silk fabric that they had donated. The kimonos were draped on the deities on the Radha-Krishna altar (Figure 12) and then revealed to the congregation at the auspicious early morning reception on the festival of Gaur Purnima in 2007. Although the dressmakers were happy, after images of the altar were circulated rumblings of dissatisfaction occurred, indicative of a wider theological and political debate (Mohan 2017b), and so the garments were never used again on the deities. Key to this debate were the circulation of deity images and the manner by which they were perceived in a different location; that is, in this case the *darshanic* quality of the altar could not be translated via digital images, and the garments could not territorialize the community as an anticipated tribute to East Asian devotees.

Another way to analyze the failure of the kimonos is to consider them from the lens of semiotic excess and slippage. The devotee makers aspired to acknowledge and inspire ISKCON's Chinese devotees by using the floral fabric that was from China as well as using a vaguely East Asian silhouette that they labeled a "kimono." Knowing that such images would circulate around the world, they seemed to have aspired to using the *darshan* images of the deity as a form of soft power that would signal to the East Asian devotees their importance within the organization. In doing so, they were apparently using the garments and deity images for their representational and semiotic qualities, using the modality of mimicry and imitation—that is, using imagery as a

FIGURE 12   Photo of Krishna and Radha in kimono outfits on the sewing room wall.
            MAYAPUR, 2012. IMAGE BY AUTHOR

form of partial presence. Yet, as Flood (2009: 75) notes, to be effective "mimicry must constantly produce its slippage, its excess, its difference." Part of the
slippage in this case was the fact that the kimono garments were relegated for
use on mannequins, placed in tableaux on the platform in front of the deity
altars. The Mayapur temple had mastered the art of creating several of these

little vignettes, grouped in a way that illustrated the theme of the altar on festival days. These vignettes generally served to mark the important days on the
Vaishnav ritual calendar, such as Damodarastaka, the festival in October and
November when the infant Krishna is celebrated. At this time a tableau of a
naughty Krishna tied to a grinding stone and being chastised by his foster-
mother Yashoda is placed on the Mayapur temple altar, and devotees sing
poignant *kirtans* to remember and celebrate the mood of this *leela*. One year
a kimono garment was seen to be reused, flattened, and draped to create a
clumsy sari-like dress for the mannequin of mother Yashoda. Too important
to be merely discarded from the temple and yet too controversial to be used
on the deities, the kimonos were turned into yardage, valued for their fabric
and pretty patterns but not for their silhouettes or their production. While
such events remind us of the perceived inappropriateness of the kimonos on a
global stage, their disuse (and reuse) emphasizes how such objects and images
constantly slip from one register to another, from the local to the global and
vice versa, even while being incorporated within the auspices of *darshan* and
temple worship.

Such three-dimensional props and installations also relate to the concept of
jhanki, not so much as a brief glimpse of the deity but as a view of a motionless
tableau vivant much like one might see in such ritual performances as Rasleela
and Ramleela in parts of northern India (Luchesi 2015). One of the deities worshipped in the Mayapur temple is Narasimha, an incarnation of Vishnu as a
man-lion. Historical uses of the Narasimha image suggest that its symbolism
has been reframed at different times to suit prevailing needs, further resonating the liminality of a deity who is half-man and half-lion and whose protective image is placed in liminal spaces such as doorways. In a colonial account,
the missionary-turned-historian Edward Thompson describes an image of
Narasimha. He notes that in a Bengali town, "in the very centre of the Bazaar,
the vegetable market, appeared a 30-feet-high image of Vishnu in his man-lion
incarnation, tearing out the bowels of a figure flung face upwards across his
knees. The figure was pale-complexioned and dressed like an Englishman"
(Thompson 1930: 90 in Pinney 2009: 32). The tableau also featured Gandhi and
the Ali Brothers,[26] Mother India, and a cow gazing adoringly at the deity. The
image described by Thompson is clearly a depiction of Narasimha disembow-
eling colonial power embodied in the English soldier while nationalist figures
such as Gandhi look on in approval. Such three-dimensional figures helped

---

26   Maulana Shaukat Ali (1873–1938 CE) and Maulana Muhammad Ali (1878–1931 CE), both
      leading figures in the Indian Muslim nationalist movement and the Khilafat Movement
      to restore the Sunni caliph of the Ottoman Caliphate.

to generate images that were "able to occupy such prominent public spaces because of their double coding; when accused of politicality they could seek refuge in the mythic" (ibid.). The overtly nationalistic use of images is absent in Mayapur, but this example does suggest that the use of tableaux was, and still is, an important semiotic device in Bengal that nondiscursively negotiates the changing needs of the community.

The tableaux that surrounds the Mayapur altar on most festival days resonates the manner in which Durga Puja is celebrated in Bengal, and, indeed, clay artisans who work on Puja figures are sometimes invited to mold decorations for the temple. As part of the discussion of imagery, one might wonder what effects ISKCON's presence (and success) has on local imaginations. The Durga Puja festival is the biggest Hindu festival celebrated throughout the state of West Bengal and marks the victory of Goddess Durga over the evil buffalo-demon Mahishasura, thus epitomizing the victory of good over evil. (Nowadays, corporate sponsors are also involved, and both money and prestige are at stake when they are innovating new themes and designs.) In this scenario, one of the ways in which ISKCON has fed into local imagery is as a theme for a Durga Puja *pandal* (pavilion) and through recreations of the monumental Temple of Vedic Planetarium (TOVP). Although incomplete at the time of writing, the temple has inspired the villages around Mayapur.

One *pandal* in the town of Jirat involved a cloth and a bamboo façade built over four months with inspiration from computer graphic images of the TOVP, available online. The interior of the *pandal* creatively used elements from the existing Prabhupada Pushpa Samadhi a memorial to Prabhupada in Mayapur. Inspired by visits to the memorial and the internet, a club member had spent three weeks replicating the mosaic design from the ceiling of the Samadhi, which featured scenes from Prabhupada's life. Painted clay figures of pale-skinned celibate initiates, or *brahmacharis*, playing musical instruments were stationed around the room and referenced the golden statues that adorned the roof of the Samadhi. Inside the *pandal*, visitors paid their respects before the deities of Durga and her family and then transferred their attention to the colorful ceiling. The deities too formed part of the ISKCON theme: a hastily painted and adorned clay figure of Krishna as a child was seated in the front of the altar. Inverting the logic of the Krishna-Kali print that was discussed earlier, the Jirat altar catered to a different non-Vaishnav audience and showcased Durga's physical and emotional efficacy and strength. Beautifully carved and painted, Durga in all her finery radiated over the vanquished buffalo-demon as a protective force, while the presence of Krishna seemed more of an afterthought. Although interested to hear of such phenomena (and participating in them to a lesser extent), ISKCON devotees themselves are skeptical about how long the influence of the TOVP will last on such events. Some speculated that the same people who had spent so much time re-creating the atmosphere of an ISKCON temple would probably choose another Hindu sect to imitate the following year. The main incentive of setting up pavilions for Durga Puja was to win competitions, and each neighborhood tried to outdo the other by coming up with something new. As discussed earlier in this monograph in the context of the goddess Jagaddhatri, Durga Puja rituals are innovative, and the inclusion or exclusion of deities in a pavilion is indicative of changing beliefs as well as historical conditions. Similarly, one might understand the inclusion of Krishna in a pavilion as testimony to wider social changes wherein ISKCON has carved a space for itself in the twenty-first-century Bengali religioscape as a group that is wealthy and successful.

As in the case of most religious consumption, the need exists to produce new images or new versions of a theme for the devotional market. Jain (2007: 205) points out the paradox of newness in such devotional images when she comments on the need to balance novelty with iconographic recognizability. Artists and printers observe that very little can be different in pictures of gods and goddesses; since the subject remains the same, the only things that can be changed are the colors and the dress. As seen in the use of multihued devotional prints and photographs often featuring attractively dressed Hindu deities, color is essential to devotional encounters. Many Hindu temples have a well-established history of deity images being quickly adapted to traditional worship practices as well as to newer technologies such as photography and offset printing. The "new" in this context is certainly welcome and auspicious but also has to be qualified as the paradoxical need for something that is *both* different and the same. For example, the image of Balagopal (Child Krishna) is a popular one, especially in domestic worship. The same image of the chubby, mischievous toddler caught in the act of eating stolen butter is used and re-used with minor variations while ensuring that the basic elements remains unchanged. Similar images can be found in different areas, used by spatially dislocated but visually connected audiences. Thus a sweet-shop owner in the city of Puri, Odisha, a visitor to Mayapur, West Bengal, and a diasporic Indian living in Dubai, U.A.E. (Figure 13) can all own and consume the same image of Balagopal in slightly different ways. The shop owner places the deity image on the door at the entry way to his store and is clearly engaged in dressing and worshipping it. As seen in the photo, the forehead of the deity bears marks of red *sindur* powder, and a cloth skirt dresses the frame with marigolds tucked in as offerings. In Mayapur, the young boy who purchases and wears the red T-shirt with NatCut Krishna printed on the front may attempt to live up to the English transliteration of the Hindi word *natkhat* (naughty). And, finally, the third image in Figure 13 is a detail of the expensive, lenticular poster that I saw during a trip to Dubai where there is a large Indian population and ISKCON

FIGURE 13   (Left to right) *Murti* in a store in Puri; T-shirt in Mayapur; poster in Dubai.
IMAGE BY AUTHOR

is engaged in active outreach efforts. The poster detail depicts baby Krishna with his hand moving as if in the act of feeding himself some stolen butter. The owner of this poster was a pious Vaishnavite who had purchased it from an ISKCON temple in India. She was happy to include it within her urban altar room along with other religious images and paraphernalia, and glad to show it to me as something novel (and yet the same).

9   Dressing for the Deities

Indic garments are both physical and metaphysical entities that transform and balance the wearer's contents, qualities, and relationships. Their performative value is supplemented by beliefs and practices based on cloth as a transmitter of "bio-moral" energy that alters the wearer's nature and does "not symbol- ise a status acquired by other means" but is "an essential component of the very transformation itself" (Bayly 1986: 287). Yet, studies that focus on religious clothing (Arthur 2000; Hume 2013) tend to equate the abilities of garments and accessories with what they symbolize, whereas those on Indian fashion (Sandhu 2015; Wilkinson-Weber 2014) assume that garments cover or resurface an individual to represent identity as a meaning or affiliation. This is an under- lying assumption that is found in other studies of clothing and decoration in the West as well.[27] However, clothing does much more than signal identity and

27   For examples see Brett 2005; Brydon and Niessen, eds. 1998; Entwistle and Wilson, eds. 2001; Guy, Banim and Green, eds. 2001; Niessen, ed. 2003; Paulicelli and Clark, eds. 2009.

possesses "translational" (Küchler and Were, eds. 2005: xxii) and transformative capabilities that influence the wearer.

Positive transformation in the devotional context of ISKCON is the progressive refinement of oneself at the particulate level by using substances in "right
eating, right marriage, and other right exchanges and actions" (Marriott and
Inden 1977: 233). These practices are governed by rules or religio-moral codes
(*dharma*) of substance and conduct[28] and vice versa. ISKCON has attempted
to revive the caste system as *varnashram dharma*—that is, the religio-moral
categorization of persons according to their qualities and propensities. It has
drawn on its *bhakti* roots to welcome personalized devotion as well as being
unorthodox in converting foreigners into the caste system. Simultaneously, it
attempts to create its own orthopraxy by standardizing practices such as clothing. In a normative framework, clothing for Brahmin men (in this case, all men
initiated into ISKCON) would indicate their social status during the four stages
of life or *ashrams*. A Brahmin man would grow from a celibate student (*brah-
machari*) to a married householder (*grihastha*), retiree, or forest dweller (*vana-
prastha*) and finally to a renunciate (*sanyasi*).

The guidelines sent to new residents of Mayapur provide advice on garments to be worn while they are living in the sacred place (*dham*). For women,
"chastely worn saris, gopi skirts with appropriately draped dupatta, and Punjabi
suits are appropriate in public areas. Petticoats or skirts, which look like petticoats, would be seen as underwear in India and thus are not proper attire
for public wear. Ladies should keep their hair tied, not loose. Married ladies
should wear red bindi." For men, "dhotis, kurtas or long pants are proper attire.
No lungis. Western attire should be avoided in the Dhama (i.e., singlets, jeans,
shorts, T-shirts with mundane or offensive logos, etc.)."[29] Leslie (1993: 202) es-
sentializes the role of gender norms in Hindu clothing and states that the types
of clothing prohibitions and injunctions for women in Hinduism are different
from those for men, as their goals differ. The devotion of men, she says, is di-
rected toward the divine, whereas the devotion of women is channeled toward
their husbands as divinity.

While it would be incorrect to simply assume that Hindu women dress
primarily for their husband, it is worth looking at the social injunctions on
women's clothing within devotional communities as part of an "invention of
tradition" (Hobsbawm and Ranger 1983: 4–5) in the nineteenth and twentieth

---

28 In his study of medieval Bengali social norms and relations, Inden (1976: 21) observes that
    dhatu (substance) and *dharma* (codes of action and conduct) are of one etymology (dhr)
    thereby etymologically supporting the non-dualism of what he terms "substance-codes."

29 Personal email communication, 29 May 2012.

centuries. ISKCON is a revitalization movement that claims to revitalize authentic values and practices in a modern age. The reframing of a sari as a Vedic garment to be worn by a Vaishnav woman attempts to strengthen the association between femininity, virtue, and tradition. (The option of the *gopi* skirt, a long flowing skirt such as might have been worn by the milkmaids in Vrindavan, is also qualified for modesty by the need for a *dupatta* or scarf to be draped appropriately around the head and chest.) In this sense, ISKCON's practices also harken back to the nineteenth-century influence of genteel, or *bhadralok*, culture in Bengal and other parts of India, when women began to wear regional drapes with blouses, shoes, and petticoats (Tarlo 1996: 28, 46). The sari also carried a symbolic weight in Hindu mythology, colonial Bengal, and the creation of the Indian nation-state (Ramaswamy 2010; Tarlo 1996; Tu 2009), and the formerly regional drape of the *nivi* became a national style in India following independence from the British.

The sari is imbued with the value of a certain manner of wearing, carrying, and inhabiting the garment and the ability to move, literally and metaphorically, in the field of a religious *habitus*, or what Bourdieu in his study of social practice called "systems of durable, transposable dispositions" (1990: 53). To be perpetuated as an ideal garment and territorialize values of South Asian femininity as spiritual ones, the sari in ISKCON relies on a combination of social norms, practice, and belief in an Indic transactional concept of persons as substances. The perceived need for devotee women to dress gracefully and modesty is bolstered by events from mythology as well as the cultural views of devotees. Models for the ISKCON woman as an ideal bride/wife include characters from the *Ramayana*, such as Sita, lauded for her unwavering devotion to her husband, Ram, and, of course, the *gopis* (milkmaids) celebrated for their devotion to Krishna. The image of the disrobed woman is highly evocative, partly because of its role in the epic *Mahabharata* in the famous incident where Duryodhana disrobes Draupadi. This event has subsequently become a common trope in Indian films, literature, and art; see Figure 14 for an example of this theme in lithographic art.

In the *Mahabharata*, Krishna is credited with the miracle of creating an unending sari that protects Draupadi's virtue. An unusual reference to this incident (Ganguly 1979: 108) moves our focus away from the event as a site of transcendental intervention toward a bodily technique called *vastra gopana*, one of the sixty-four classical arts, or *kalas. Vastra gopana* ("garment protection" in Sanskrit) is described as the art of covering oneself with a garment so that it does not slip off the body with movement or wind and invokes the value of bodily motions and gestures required to keep a sari wrapped around oneself. Such an interpretation of sari use in mythology invites a more nuanced

FIGURE 14   *Draupadi Vastraharan*, Lithograph, 1920s, Ravi Verma Press, Lonavla.
IMAGE COURTESY OF CHRISTOPHER PINNEY

consideration of how the garment is used and manipulated in everyday life. Analyzing the sari through the art of wrapping and contexts of covering/revealing allows us to emphasize the wearer's skill and to consider the garment as not only a symbol of feminine modesty but also a performance.

We have previously considered the importance of *rasa* or aesthetic experience in ISKCON, and this can be extended from a worship context to the daily motions and techniques of the body as factored into wearing the sari (Banerjee and Miller 2003). According to one devotee, a middle-aged European woman who was used to wearing both Indian and Western styles of clothing, the type of clothing greatly influences a person's mood. A sari or simply a length of garment such as a *dupatta* (scarf) can be draped in different ways to flow around the body, thereby influencing the aesthetics of the wearer's interactions with others. When draped improperly or worn by somebody who lacks appropriate behavior and bodily conduct, the sari and its wearer can potentially become clumsy or unsocial. In this context, the properly socialized Vaishnavi was therefore mindful of using the physical properties of the sari and her practical knowledge to manipulate the garment, creating a suitable mood of grace and elegance and thereby influencing the manner in which she was perceived. For instance, the woman at the altar in Figure 15 is approaching the small deities of Gaur-Nitai (Chaitanya and his brother) to perform a ritual ablution using the shell in her hand as a dispenser. The women around her are already modeling the behavior expected from devotee women by making sure their sari has been pulled up at least partly over their heads, as a sign of modesty and respect for the deities. As she approaches the deities in order to pour the contents of the shell over them the woman in the blue saree pulls up the saree end over her head. The extent to which the saree covers a woman's head and how tightly it is wrapped can also signal something about the wearer's character and her desire (and ability) to conform to a certain perception of modesty and sanctity. According to some women, the sari is also capable of acting as a form of protection that ensures that others interact suitably with the wearer. Thus a devotional sari, if one could term it that, influences and constrains the behavior of both the wearer and others toward rectitude and restraint.

Another aspect of the devotional garment is the manner in which it intersects with flows of modernity and globality. For instance, bridal fashion trends find their way into ISKCON weddings with costumes that are made in "ethnic chic" style. Although until the 1990s ethnic elements were not popular, the subsequent growing globalization and economic liberalization of India has been connected to the development of an urban middle class and its consumer culture (Brosius 2011). As part of the same cultural phenomenon as the reclaiming of heritage by young and upwardly mobile Indians, many of ISKCON's young

FIGURE 15   A woman adjusting her sari so that it covers her head while performing a ritual
             ablution for the deities.
             MAYAPUR, 2013. IMAGE BY AUTHOR

foreign and Indian devotees look at prevailing ethnic and regional dress styles
when designing their wedding garments. In such cases, they combine the idea
of a traditionally themed wedding with Krishna Consciousness and the emphasis that the wedding be conducted at an ISKCON temple or associated fa-
cility. One such wedding near Mayapur was accompanied by the designing of
custom outfits, using fabric and embellishments from stores in Kolkata. The
sketch in Figure 16 is an example of how a wedding dress might be designed in
the style of a *gaghra-choli-odhani* (skirt, blouse, and veil) with attention paid to
the style of the blouse and the attachment of borders. Such devotee-designers
pay attention to national fashion trends, including Bollywood (the Hindu film
industry), and combine them with preexisting expertise in making and sourc-
ing embroidered *zardozi* trims, patches, and yardage. Although the foreign
devotees who wear such clothing may not consider themselves as Indian or
even Hindu (ascribing instead to a worship of Krishna that transcends Indian
nationality and any definitions of Hinduism), their clothing choices at weddings can be heavily influenced by Indian bridal clothing trends. For example,

FIGURE 16   Sketch for devotee's wedding dress.
MAYAPUR, 2013. IMAGE BY AUTHOR

wedding outfits may be influenced by the costumes of actors in Hindi films, such as *Jodha Akbar*,[30] that depict romantic themes of Indian majesty. In this respect, while stressing the modesty and plain dress of women devotees, a wedding is one of the occasions in which devotional dress and embellished clothing are combined as appropriate, if not auspicious.

Rituals of passage (*samskaras*) such as weddings, pregnancy, and childbirth are important, transformational events, and the wearing of talismanic accessories, such as amulets, helps tide the devotee through this transition.[31] In a study of categories of kinship among Bengali Hindus and Muslims in both India and Bangladesh, ethnosociologists (Inden and Nicholas 1977) noted that when a

---

30   *Jodha Akbar* is a quasihistorical film, released in 2008, that recounts the romance between the Mughal king Akbar and his Hindu wife Jodha.

31   The *Sat kriya sara dipika*, a Gaudiya Vaishnav manual by Gopala Bhatta Goswami, one of Chaitanya's followers, describes 16 *samskaras*, but devotees in Mayapur, as do most Bengalis, emphasize ten transformative rites: *Vivaha karma* (marriage), *Garbhadana* (conception), *Jata karma* (birth ceremony), *Niskramanam* (taking the child outside for the first time), *Nama karana* (name-giving ceremony), *Paustika karma* (continued health of child), *Anna prasana* (first grain's ceremony), *Chuda karanam* (hair-cutting ceremony), *Upanayana* (thread ceremony and rites of a Brahmin), and *Samavartana* (graduation ceremony).

Bengali woman marries, her body as well as her inborn code for conduct is thought to be transformed. The bride became a wife in that family by acquiring a new *dharma*, as a wife in the new kin group of her husband. Thus *samskaras* are believed to prepare and purify and to literally make the individual anew. During such a powerful process, pregnant women and children are considered especially vulnerable to disembodied spirits and evil forces.

During the *simantonnayanam*, or hair-parting ceremony to protect a pregnant woman, the husband ties an herbal *kavacha* around his wife's neck to ward off spirits that threaten the fetus. The word *kavacha* means "armor" in Sanskrit[32] and has its origins in the properties of small pouches made from herbs and plants. In general, devotees wear *kavachas* on their upper arms and necks in the form of tiny metal containers (mostly silver) with auspicious material placed inside. The material in a Narasimha *kavacha*, for example, could consist of a prayer invoking the 108 names of the deity and some *prasad* in the form of dried flowers or leaves from an offering to the Narasimha deity at the Mayapur temple. Other devotees simply attach a small twig of neem, a medicinal wood, to their upper arm with string as a temporary *kavacha*.

Young children are also considered vulnerable; one Bengali mother of a three-year-old son (Figure 17) made him wear a Narasimha *kavacha*, because she firmly believed that if the child were face to face with danger, the deity would be his only protection. Devotees also wore the *kantimala*, or choker, a string of holy basil beads believed to purify the throat (*kanti*) and the voice as one practices chanting. (Some believed that, similar to a dog collar that warned others that the dog was owned by somebody and hence not just a stray, the neck choker warned Yama, the god of death, that a devotee's soul was under the protection of his or her master, Krishna.) *Kantimalas* are worn as one, two, or three strands of beads, and devotees who have taken their second initiation[33] must wear either a two- or a three-strand *mala*. Bengali parents often combined the *kantimala* and *kavacha* with the folk practice of a black spot on the face that was believed to ward off the evil eye. Of course, these devotional paraphernalia do not work in isolation but are combined with other bodily markers to make up the totality of devotional dress. For instance, the woman in Figure 17 is a Bengali *zardozi* embroiderer whose husband works in the Mayapur temple's

---

32   Monier-Williams (2005 [1872]), *A Sanskrit-English Dictionary*, p. 264. *Kavacha* refers to "armour ... a coat of mail ... any covering; a corset, jacket ... a piece of bark or birch-leaf or any substance inscribed with mystical words and carried about as an amulet.".

33   The second initiation, or *siksha* (education), is normally carried out a couple years after the first initiation called *diksha*, and, following this, the devotee is considered a twice-born, or *Brahmin*. The guru who provides the second initiation is called the *siksha* guru and will guide the disciple through his or her practice and life.

FIGURE 17   A Bengali devotee and her son wear *kantimala* strands with metal *kavachas*.
MAYAPUR, 2013. IMAGE BY AUTHOR

sewing room. (She and her husband also work on embroidery orders for devotees from their home.) Accompanied by her young son, she is seated in front
of her embroidery frame at home and wears the *kantimala* and *kavacha* with a
tilak marking on her forehead. She also wears the typical Bengali red lac (*pola*)
and white conch (*sankha*) bangles as well as red powder (*sindur*) in her hair
parting that indicates that she is a married woman.

In addition to clothing and paraphernalia, one can also consider body markings as forms of dress. Men and women apply auspicious *tilaks*, or markings,
on twelve parts of the body daily using a paste called *gopi-chandana*, made
from the sacred soil of Vrindavan or Dwaraka, where the deities are believed
to have walked and played. The form of the tilak symbolizes Vishnu's foot and
shows that the devotee has surrendered him- or herself at the feet of the deity.
While chanting purificatory mantras the devotee applies the tilak on twelve
different parts of the body: forehead, stomach, chest, throat, right side, right
upper arm, right shoulder, left side, left upper arm, left shoulder, upper back,
and lower back. Many devotees also tattoo their bodies with tilaks in a manner

that echoes the traditional branding of religious symbols on the skin in other schools of Vaishnavism.[34]

As we have seen, norms are implemented in ISKCON through clothing ranging from cloth to beads to substances. One of the ways in which such religio-moral codes can be traced is through the choice of fabric and the way devotees harness the relative porosity of bodies and cloths as conductors of substance-codes. The porosity of the Hindu body and its vulnerability through contact is a quality that is also used to maintain or elevate the substance of the devotee. Ideally, an ISKCON Brahmin would make continuous adjustments to his or her person through regulatory practices meant to refine and improve bodily substance and nature. For instance, touching a spiritualized entity (whether an object or a person) refines the participant such that any contact with that entity can be elevating. At home devotees exhibit and worship garments (or rather their fragments) worn by a beloved guru. Some occasionally drape a deity's garment—perhaps a skirt that was torn and procured as *prasad*—or tie a piece of sanctified thread or fabric around their wrist. It is believed that physically touching these fabrics can transfer some of their auspicious substance. Bodily secretions would normally be considered extremely polluting, but this logic is inverted in the case of a spiritualized entity whether a guru or deity.

Although clothing norms seem rigid and overarching, they lend themselves to negotiations in exigent situations governed by *upadharma*, or "a bylaw, a secondary or minor religious precept."[35] Consider the resistive property of certain fabrics. Synthetic materials, while permissible for footwear, are inappropriate for ritual contexts since they cannot be purified by any means. The explanation given by devotees is that all synthetics are made from plastic or oil and are resistant to cleansing by water, sun, moon, and air. This is also the reason why devotees should ideally not wear synthetic fabrics such as nylon or sit on plastic mats when performing their daily worship. Although the impenetrability of synthetics is bad for ritual purposes, a partly resistant fabric such as silk or wool can be useful for that very same quality in a different context. A drop of water on wool will bead and is not quickly absorbed; thus wool by its nature does not become contaminated by air or touch and (although resistant to cleansing by water) can be purified by wind, sun, or moon. For instance,

---

34   Schools of Vaishnavism, such as the Madhava and Sri *sampradayas*, or lineages, used to practice the branding of religious symbols, including Vishnu's wheel and Ram's name, on the bodies of initiates.

35   See https://dsalsrv04.uchicago.edu/cgi-bin/app/apte_query.py?page=448, last accessed 16 April 2019.

to avoid pollution, young boys in the *gurukul* (school) may wear a wool blanket, or *chadar*, instead of their cotton *dhoti* while going to the toilet. Another example of negotiating pollution is the dilemma of whether women priests should continue their devotional service during their monthly period, when they are considered impure (*muchi*), especially if nobody else is available. Here *upadharma* comes into action, and because of the emphasis on uninterrupted service to Krishna, the woman priest (*pujari*) must perform the *puja*. The priest would wear a silk sari instead of cotton while performing the *puja*, since silk acts as a buffer that prevents her "contaminating" substance from being transmitted to the deity.

According to Gaudiya Vaishnav philosophy, in the age of *kali* everybody is born a *shudra* (untouchable) and, regardless of caste, needs reformation to become a Brahmin. Since all initiated devotees in ISKCON are considered to be Brahmins, the sacred thread worn by men indicates that status alone and not those of the Kshatriya and Vaishya castes.[36] Perhaps the most important element for male devotees is the sacred thread (*upavita*). After the sacred thread, the loincloth (*kaupina*) worn by ascetics is an essential symbol of purity through control and sexual abstinence and is believed to hold in the positive substance and strength of semen. The *kaupina* is considered worshipable for *sanyasis* and represents the vow of chastity and renunciation.[37] It is said that when one of Chaitanya's disciples, Gopala Bhatta Goswami, left the sacred town of Puri, Chaitanya sent his *kaupina* with him as a worshipable embodiment of himself. Even today a guru's substance is considered sacred, and devotees may keep a pair of their guru's footwear or clothing in their homes for worship.[38] For example, the personal belongings and clothing of a deceased ISKCON guru, Sridhar Swami, are displayed in a case in the Radha Rasabihari temple in Juhu, Mumbai. The items include ochre garments that signify his status as a renunciate. While this commemorative exhibit uses elements of

36   Generally, the sacred thread and the cloth worn on the upper body symbolize spiritual qualification and initiation into the twice born (*dvija*) status of the three superior castes (*varnas*).

37   For men, the value of purity is reflected in the importance of the loincloth (*langoti, kaupina*) as an essential symbol of ascetic identity in Hinduism. For women, the *Stridharmapaddhathi*, or "Guide to the Religious Status and Duties of Women," an eighteenth-century text, outlines the eternally valid norms for orthodox Hindu women. Similarly, for men there is an underlying need to maintain one's purity in order to uphold the moral-religious order, or *dharma*.

38   In one instance I saw, framed and displayed as part of a home's decoration, a tiny piece of cloth that had been used by Prabhupada. The small size indicated that it had been cut from a larger piece of fabric and that perhaps many devotees had acquired similar such pieces.

museum display such as the glass case and labels, the items are considered *prasad* and have a spiritual potency that arises from the substance of the guru, his location within a lineage or *parampara* of Vaishnav gurus, and his complete surrender to his guru—the founder Prabhupada—that is evoked by the cap embroidered with the words "Prabhupada's Dog."

Sanyasis and *brahmacharis*—that is, those who have taken vows of renunciation and celibacy—wear two pieces of unsewn cloth, one to cover the upper part of the body (*uttara, chadar*) and one to cover the lower part of the body (*dhoti*). Cut and sewn cloth is considered damaged (*ahata*), and men taking part in rituals may wear only a woven upper cloth instead of a sewn *kurta*. The color of clothing varies from saffron for *brahmacharis* and *sanyasis* to white/multicolored for *grihasthas*, or householders (Figure 18). The deities' names, whether in sonic or visual form, should not be damaged or distorted, and it is advised that clothing incorporate the symbols and text depicting the deities' names in their whole form. Despite this advice, devotional stores in Mayapur, Vrindavan, and Puri sell printed shirts and *kurtas* made of preprinted fabric with sacred symbols such as Vishnu's *chakra* (wheel) and conch and the words of the *mahamantra*. Printed *uttaras* in white and saffron may also be worn for ritual occasions, although the printing is preferably done after the fabric has been cut. *Dhotis* are draped in the North Indian style with variation in the final presentation based on the occasion and pattern and crispness of the fabric. Leather products are banned, and so, for footwear, devotees can choose between wooden or synthetic shoes. Synthetic footwear is very popular for its functionality, and styles range from those that resemble wooden *padukas* to imitation Croc sandals, which are practical in Mayapur's muddy terrain.

C. A. Bayly (1986) suggests some basic uses of cloth in Hindu society that are applicable in this context. They include cloth's ability to symbolize or record changes of status as well as its magical or "transformative" use, whereby the moral and physical being of the wearer/recipient are believed to be actually changed by the innate qualities and substance of the cloth. In ISKCON, garments such as Indian-style saris, *kurtas*, and *dhotis* are worn by initiates, priests, and lay devotees, and an appropriate subjectivity is ensured partly through the control of the body by cloth's physical and metaphysical properties. Such garments are intended to facilitate a universal Krishna-centered identity and, as a uniform does, help to identify devotees to outsiders as well as transcend the boundaries of race, ethnicity, and nationality within the group (Prabhupada 1983: 183, 298). However, clothing values are not just about dressing norms and identifying oneself to others; they can also be related to the efficacy of paraphernalia and practices. Since the code for conduct of living persons is immanent in bodily substance and not transcendent, the body can be manipulated

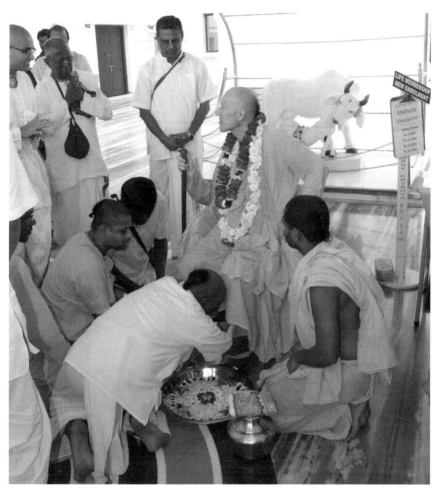

FIGURE 18   Devotees comprising householders and *brahmacharis* gather around a guru.
            CHENNAI, 2012. IMAGE BY AUTHOR

through the formal and aesthetic aspects of garments, such as via the color and
type of clothing, the absence/presence of ornaments and decoration, and associated bodily practices such as applying markings and chanting.

10   Chanting as Devotional Technique

As ISKCON's injunctions state, a devotee must engage in regulatory practices
such as chanting on prayer beads (*japamala*). This process is meant to move
the devotee progressively away from the worldly toward the otherworldly. The

japamala, or prayer beads, (hereafter referred to as *mala*) is a meditational device that regulates the body, mind, and senses and is considered essential to devotional practice (*sadhana*). It is believed that chanting the *mahamantra*, a process called *nama japa*, is the only way people in *kali yuga* (the current age in the Hindu cosmic cycle) can achieve liberation. Chanting is an activity that accompanies an individual from birth to death—a baby born into the community hears the sounds of chanting through infancy. Subsequently, the young child acquires and handles beads and bead bags, laying the foundation for a lifetime of practice. As a devotee dies, the sounds of chanting accompany the process of what is believed to be the departure of the soul from the body. Given the prevalence of chanting in ISKCON, I explore it here as a religious bodily technique that makes and sustains certain kinds of connections.

The design of a *mala* is simple and consists of a number of beads threaded along a long length of twine with a knot between each bead. The knot ensures that the beads stay in place and also, in the case of smaller beads, provides space for the fingers to grip and manipulate the bead. Most *malas* have 108 beads, but smaller, wrist-sized *malas* with 27 or 54 beads are made for travelers. The beads have to be counted several times (four times for 27 beads, two times for 54 beads) to make up a full set of 108 mantra repetitions. To help facilitate the counting of the rounds, devotees may use counting beads (*sakshimala*, or witness beads), 20 *tulasi*, rosewood, glass, or plastic beads on a separate string held in the other hand or attached to a bead bag. The design of the *mala* lends itself to being inexpensive, portable, and usable for a cross-section of devotees; its use requires little education other than the ability to memorize and chant the *mahamantra*.

Malas are generally carried in bags; the devotee usually inserts the right hand in the bag, with the index finger protruding from the bag, and begins to rotate the beads chanting *Hare Krishna, Hare Krishna, Krishna Krishna, Hare Hare, Hare Ram, Hare Ram, Ram Ram, Hare Hare,* at every bead, repeating this process 107 times more to complete a round. The *mala* can rest on the middle or ring finger of the right hand, with the beads being drawn with the help of the thumb toward the palm. Chanting is performed using only 108 of the 109 beads; the head bead is never used or crossed over. Instead it marks the beginning and end of one round of chanting. So, although there is a start or finish to each round, this status is not associated with a particular bead but is marked by the sequence of chanting. The bead that forms the end of one round of chanting (or bead 108) forms the beginning of the next round (bead 1) as the chanter simply turns the *mala* and proceeds to chant a new round by proceeding in a direction opposite to the earlier round. The *sakshimala* helps to keep track of the sixteen rounds to be chanted daily, and a new bead is moved down the string with each completed round. Four extra beads are provided if the chanter wishes to use them to mark one set of sixteen rounds, or one *granthi* ("knot" or "junction" in Sanskrit). An initiate is expected to chant sixteen rounds a day; "fixed" devotees are said to chant one *nirbandha* a day. Devotees report initially taking ten minutes to chant a round, then progressing to about seven minutes per round.

Sound in Hinduism is sacred since it is believed to emanate from the cosmic root vibration (*nada brahman*). Words can be arrangements of sacred sounds, and deities are embodied in specific mantras. By using the *mala* and chanting the *mahamantra* in the vocative case, the devotee directly invokes Krishna. The *mala* is sometimes accompanied by items of clothing, such as printed cloths, that would be draped around devotees during a ceremony, such as a first initiation (*diksha*) into ISKCON. Mantras do not necessarily require comprehension. Yet, to assume that chanting is only an automatic recitation would be incorrect. The seemingly mechanical aspect of chanting is balanced by the emphasis that one chants with emotion and imagination. Breathing rhythms are normally unconscious patterns. Chanting, however, forces devotees to become aware of breathing habits and rhythms through an emphasis on proper posture, speed of recitation, and pauses for inhalation/exhalation. The chanter also regulates the intensity and pitch of his or her recitation to use an optimum amount of energy, often resulting in a monotonal invocation. Unlike other forms of chanting, such as the Byzantine rosary, for which devotees may choose the words that they chant on a particular day (De Abreu 2008: 65), *japa* must be done with a specific mantra. The chanter develops a disciplined, repetitive practice around the structure of the *mahamantra* supported by the correlation between the number of beads and the number of times the mantra is repeated. Such relationships are not just symbolic but can serve as further means of harmonization through time, repetition, and rhythm.

A physiological experiment on the chanting of mantras monitored the electrocardiogram, respiration, and blood pressure of subjects. Recordings were made of spontaneous breathing and controlled breathing as well as free talking and recitation. The subjects had been instructed to "repeat the mantra with an 'alive' resonant voice; to listen to the sound produced and to let it *flow freely*; and then to complete the expiration comfortably after the end of the mantra" (Bernardi et al. 2001: 1447) (emphasis mine). The recitation of the beads/mantras was proven to be a lengthy activity with effects such as lowered respiratory rate, improved concentration, and increased calmness. The experiment also noted that if respiration was stabilized to a constant frequency and if this number coincided with cardiovascular rhythms, these rhythms were enhanced. This effect suggests that breathing and cardiovascular rhythms could be synchronized through chanting to create the experience of peace, calm, and clarity that some ISKCON devotees report. So what we have here is not just the mediation of inside and outside through the exchange of breath but also the results of such an exchange—that is, the transformation of the body's physiological and mental state through coordination of respiratory and cardiovascular systems.

Chanting also relies on haptic stimuli, whereby repetitive gestures with small objects have been deemed to accompany states of meditation or reverie in many religions, and the aesthetics of an intimate object, such as the *mala*, is one where "tactile perception of form is focalized and beyond which the machine of the body is entirely at rest" (Leroi-Gourhan 1993: 296). The design of the *mala* offers such an experience, because the chanter grips and slides the *mala* in a succession of discrete movements. The senses of touch, motion, hearing, and speech do not operate through separate channels but interact and create different perceptions. Experimental findings of manual haptic feedback and "haptic visuality" demonstrate how sensory inputs can be converted from one modality to another to elicit emotions and sensations in response to an object's texture, shape, and function (Jeon 2014). In addition, experiments on the differences between manual and digital haptics[39] illustrate the ability of the body to respond to the difference between active and passive forms of touch and create different perceptions. Such experiments demonstrate the embodied nature of cognition by making intention part of the stimuli involved in multisensory perception. The repeated, predictable touching of the same object is also shown to lessen neuron activity in a part of the brain that is sensitive to new stimuli. And, if the regularity of the *mala* ensures a certain rhythm and flow of motion, it is conceivable that at some point the chanter is able to move his or her attention from the act of moving beads to the pronunciation of the mantra. As devotees narrate, paying attention to their recitation also draws back the wavering and distracted mind and acts as a tool of concentration.

The processes described so far indicate that the work done by the *mala* is not just computational or mnemonic but phenomenological and praxeological, and the body of the devotional subject is the field of perception and action. The chanting body is a sensitive organ that can move between various sensory modalities to achieve a transformational balance and coherence. Through actions such as touching, handling, breathing, reciting, and listening, and the emotions and sensations that accompany them, the subject literally

---

39   In a neurocognitive experiment, an object that touches the body in passing produces a different perception than an object that the body interacts with actively and intentionally, and points to the selective nature of perception as attention (Berthoz 2000: 87).

and metaphorically feels and moves toward the divine. However, to connect this practice to devotional life, one must also consider how devotees, especially householders, constantly work to balance the normative aspects with their lives in the nondevotional world. Being a devotee for them is the struggle of aligning notions of time and space between devotional and nondevotional realms. Thus exploring the use of chanting devices also reveals some of the negotiations that ISKCON devotees must undertake to practice a global faith and how the practice of chanting is implicated.

According to Gaudiya Vaishnav, theology chanting is the supreme devotional practice and duty of this age of *kali yuga* (Holdrege 2014: 189–196). As mentioned earlier, *kali yuga* is the present age in cyclical Hindu cosmology and represents the maximum decline of morality, order, and wisdom in the world. The four *yugas* or epochs in the macrocosmic Hindu theory of time and society are *krita, treta, dwapar,* and *kali.* The *yugas* move in a cycle of repetition and progressive degeneration, with the current age of *kali* representing the most chaos and loss of coherence before the beginning of a new cosmic cycle. In ISKCON *kali yuga* is the present age that distances the devotee from Krishna, causing ontological disturbance and grief for the former. (*Japa* is meant to redress this loss by restoring the soul's connection with Krishna.) *Kali yuga* is significant in relation to India's perceived dependence on the West and Western-style consumerism, which has separated Hindus from their traditions and Krishna. *Kali yuga* is also important for Western devotees as a term that they associate with religious "voidism" and a lack of personalism in faiths such as Christianity. However, this degradation—variously invoked as dependence, loss of tradition, amnesia, and impersonalism—also provides the opportunity for redemption through *japa.* The work of the *mala* helps to detach the chanter from mundane time and attach his or her natural rhythms to the rhythms of cyclical, sacred time, also conceptualized as the *kala chakra* (wheel of time) in the Hindu cosmos.

The chanting practices of global devotees in different situations as well as technological changes, such as the use of a mechanical counter, are related to social changes and perceptions of time, indicating negotiations that accompany devotional performance within a contemporary landscape (Mohan 2016). The use of the mechanical counter, as its name indicates, is meant to increase the efficiency of counting. Efficiency is derived from the ease with which the tally can be carried in one's pocket, be easily advanced with the push of a button, and read from the dial. The counter combines the functionality of the *sakshimala* (witness or proof beads) that is used to calculate the total number of rounds and avoids the awkwardness of leaving beads hanging out of

FIGURE 19   Web page advertising the hand tally.
IMAGE BY AUTHOR

a bag or using a butterfly clip to mark one's exact position in a round. The tally is light, portable, and discreet and can be used in a variety of environments and situations. As the Krishna store website (krishnastore.com) indicates, hand tallies are sold through the site for Western customers. The web page also addresses concerns about whether it is ok to chant *japa* using the device (Figure 19), acknowledging that it is a somewhat controversial practice "but is often employed by devotees who wish to chant their rounds while commuting long distances in a vehicle, or under other circumstances where beads might be difficult or dangerous to use."

Chanting with prayer beads is an activity meant to transform the subject by regulating the mind, body, and senses as well as purifying the heart and developing a soteriological habit. By comparison, the strength of the counter is its ease and versatility of use. Following the discussion in the previous section, the push of the button does not have the same efficacy as the slide of a *mala* bead, since the kind of haptic stimulus is different and the symbolic and emotional associations of the *mala* (as an item given to a devotee by the guru at the time of initiation) are lacking in the counter. Yet, as Kratky (2012: 58) points out, the mechanical counter lowers the "cognitive load" of the computational aspect of the *mala* and frees up the mind so that the user can simultaneously complete other tasks. He observes (ibid.: 57) that by using the counter devotees in a Vienna temple[40] can chant when commuting to their workplaces, during their office jobs, and while doing housework or gardening—and that for this same reason the tally was soon banished by temple officials, who felt that it could lead to a decline and marginalization of *japa*. Similar concerns are applicable to the digital clicker which, like the counter, is portable and inconspicuous in public. However, temple regulations vary, and, in Mayapur, unlike the Vienna temple, the use of counters and clickers is allowed but is regarded as something more suitable for additional rounds (other than the daily mandated number for initiates) and for those whose work or life makes it difficult to use the *mala*, such as a mother with a young child or someone who has to commute extensively.

The use of the counter can be accommodated from a philosophical perspective, because the notion of *yukta-vairagya*[41] allows for any new technology in service of Krishna as long as its use is clearly oriented toward ISKCON's goals. However, this is not just a question of philosophy: temples have different approaches to the same issue and different ways of policing what they consider as infractions. Further, pertaining to the question of embodiment and devotion, there is also the issue of the kind of value provided by one device over another. A comparison of the counter to the *mala* indicates that the counter can be easily incorporated into, and excorporated out of, a devotee's body-schema. The counter can be used in a context, location and time-independent manner, as a counting tool, reducing the load on memory and turning the act of chanting into discrete, portable units. By doing so, it resonates the values of a postindustrial, global economy wherein people and their actions seem to have been detached from the constraints of time and space. And such a detachment brings with it different values and epistemologies of time and literacy.

Drawing a connection between the divisibility of modern time and the role of modular typesetting in the print revolution, Marshal McLuhan (in Ernst 2013: 49) notes that "only highly literate communities could imagine accepting the fragmentation of life into minutes and hours." This observation redirects our attention to the importance of print technology as a means of shaping ISKCON and Hindus in general. Figure 20 is a studio photograph from the early twentieth century that depicts how the subject, an elderly Hindu woman dressed soberly in a dark sari and blouse, wished to be portrayed. She is captured in the

---

40   Personal email communication with Jan Kratky dated 20 June 2015.
41   *Yukta* means "yoked or joined ... employed, occupied with ... prepared for ... skilful, clever, experienced in" (Monier-Williams 2005 [1872], *A Sanskrit-English Dictionary*: 853). *Vairagya* means "freedom from all worldly desires, indifference to wordly objects and to life, asceticism" (2005: 1025).

act of chanting on prayer beads with a holy book and clock in front of her as props. Publications were an important tool of dissemination in the nineteenth and twentieth centuries, propelling ISKCON's global expansion and continuing to be the backbone of its preaching efforts. Against a backdrop and history of technological adaptation, the issue of change in *japa* (and the use of the counter) is not one of modernity versus tradition but of the need to do two things simultaneously—emphasize the value of remembering Krishna in the secular world and spiritualize the act of computing. Paradoxically, a device that fits into a model of productive efficiency, such as the counter, is used to overcome these same forces in ISKCON. Other devices that are used to negotiate secular time with sacred time include the Vaishnav lunar calendars (www. vaisnavacalendar.com), that have been adapted such that instead of advocating one specific time for a religious event, dates and times are recalculated based on the temple's time zone in the world.

In engaging in a discussion of time, we have seemingly moved far from the issue of clothing. Yet we remain close to the body and questions of devotional experience and labor. Bodily paraphernalia, such as prayer beads, might also count as devotional clothing if one were to take into consideration the intimacy of these objects with the body's surface as well as the idea of the devotee as a fluid, loosely bounded "dividual" whose concerns with regulating interpersonal transactions are part of a constant negotiation of biological instability and moral risk. Part of such transactions is the transformation of the wearer's morality/code of conduct (*dharma*), qualities (*guna*), and power (*shakti*) through the practice of chanting and the movement of "coded-particles" across the osmotic boundaries of prayer beads and skin surfaces. Within this framework, we note that the actions discussed so far as part of devotional living (right eating, worship, dressmaking, chanting, and so forth) constitute the appropriate conduct (*achara*) that sustains the individual and the community (Marriott and Inden 1977: 231).

Gunas, or qualities, refer to the innate properties of the nature of humans and objects. In a cosmos conceived as a living thing where matter is alive, the primordial protoplasm is made up of these three strands—*sattva* (truth), *tamas* (destruction), and *rajas* (creation). The main trinity of Hindu divinity comprises Vishnu the preserver, Brahma the creator, and Shiva the destroyer, and each embodies the fullest expression of *sattva, rajas*, and *tamas*, respectively. *Sattva guna* also connotes values of purity, balance, and radiance and is the desired mode of life for devotees. As we noted earlier, *gunas* can be aestheticized and signified, for example, via the brilliant opulence of deity clothing that expresses a correspondence between the metaphysics of the deities' qualities of enlightenment, brightness, and goodness.

FIGURE 20   Woman with *japamala*, clock and book, 1930s, Laxmi Art Photo Studios, Mumbai.
IMAGE COURTESY OF CHRISTOPHER PINNEY

Gunas also have a relationship with time and the concept of *kali yuga*. For instance, Ramakrishna, the *bhakti* saint of the nineteenth century, used these concepts to identify and satirize genteel devotees in Bengali society. He did so to apolitically criticize the prevalence of *chakri* (clerical work), or the introduction of Western notions of discipline and time in employment that distanced people from *bhakti* (Sarkar 1997: 316). In a contemporary nonreligious context, Pinney (1999) points out the multiple valencies of *kali yuga* as *kal yuga* (age of machines) through the differing views of village factory workers and their high-caste village employers in Nagda, Madhya Pradesh.[42] Further, Inden (1976: 50) argues for the flexibility of the concept of *kali yuga* whereby it is significant not so much as an objective dateable period of time but as a subjective, relational entity that makes certain values urgent and immanent. He narrates meeting Bengali Vaishnavs who date the advent of *kali yuga* with the Muslim conquest of Bengal in the thirteenth and fourteenth centuries and the slow demise of Vaishnavism. Hence, each age, Inden argues, could be characterized as a *kali yuga* in relation to its predecessor. Today *kali yuga* in ISKCON is most significant vis-à-vis India's perceived dependence on the West and Western-style consumerism that has distanced Hindus from Krishna. This situation is often summarized by comments on the irony of Western converts who come to India searching for Krishna while Indian Hindus migrate to the West and forget him; Indians, it is said, stand close to Krishna through their birth but with their backs to him, while Western devotees are far from Krishna but face him.

If it takes a devotee anywhere between seven to ten minutes to chant one complete round of 108 mantras, then the amount of time needed to chant a daily quota of sixteen rounds is approximately two to three hours. For many devotees, especially those who live outside Mayapur, this raises questions about the sustainability of the practice, creating space to consider alternatives. Time in a postindustrial society is not the seamless, revelatory entity that it was in a religious world. Instead, time is determined by what is mathematically feasible. Correspondingly, human effort becomes a resource that can be moved or accessed anywhere. Urban devotees such as those who work for multinational corporations in India's numerous office centers must learn to alter their sleep and work rhythms to synchronize with a different time zone. Their adherence is not just to a secular clock but a global clock that forces them to adapt *japa* to their work routine. One young man who worked for a European firm in the South Indian city of Bengaluru described listening to *kirtans* in the corporate taxi that took him to work and argued that this was a form of chanting. A young mother, struggling with maintaining her chanting routine, realized that she would have to alter her chanting schedule to accommodate the needs of her new baby instead of holding onto an idea of what was ideal practice. These kinds of mental and physical negotiation were required precisely because the

---

42   For the employers, the local rayon factory represents *kali yuga* as a dangerous and unstable modernity, whereas for the workers the factory represents liberation from long working hours and oppressive, rural patronage.

rhythms of sacred time were in a conflicting relationship with secular time. Devotional practice in such cases was not merely conformity to norms but included the means by which devotees reconciled ideal states and reality.

11   Conclusion: Clothing as Efficacious Intimacy

In this monograph, I have approached devotional bodies as fluid entities, endowed with qualities but also transformable by action. Practices of right living, right dressing, right eating, and a host of other decisions regarding material choices and actions shape Hindu devotees in ISKCON, a Gaudiya Vaishnav sect, as holistic entities whose substance is inbuilt with morality. Matter is not separated from spirit, and neither is the feeling body differentiated from the spiritual body, produced through an orientation toward, and a consciousness of, the deity Krishna. Practices such as dressing oneself as a Brahmin and the collective efforts required to keep the deities *murtis* clothed opulently are important because they are believed to literally transform peoples' nature, orient them toward Krishna, and shape their soteriological destiny.

Like many Hindu sects, figuration and the physical deity form are central to ISKCON's practice of devotional love, or *bhakti.* Unlike the notion of a Hindu pantheon of large and small gods, ISKCON promotes Krishna as both, dealing with everyday phenomena of cows and babies as well as cosmic problems such as salvation in the age of *kali yuga.* The Krishna depicted in *leelas* is both the didactic hero of the *Gita* and the mischievous child of Damodarastaka. Nevertheless, this concept of being both human-like and supra-human needs to be made actionable and relatable. The altar is not just a representation of the transcendental realm but the locus of the temple's efficacy in mobilizing divine power, people, and resources. In exploring temple worship, my description started with the sensorium of *darshan* and related it to other practices such as celebratory singing, dancing, and prostration. By analyzing the experiences of devotees in the temple, it suggests that certain sensory experiences, such as the visual tactility of *darshan*, and material effects, such as the "shimmer" of deity garments, were integral to the mood of opulence in the temple. The imposition of a mood of reverence did not mean that emotions were lacking. Instead, within a sensorium of the "body-in-motion," devotees learned to form an intimacy with the deity that included respectful distance as well as energetic expression.

This monograph is oriented toward understanding Hindu devotion as a transitive, intimate entity. People use the properties and aesthetics of clothing to articulate subjecthood through self-world relations. Bodies and materials are mobilized to resonate/interfere and amplify/dampen ideas, experiences, dispositions, and concerns. The strategic use of material affordances in processes of making and use helps to activate social relations by encouraging desired aspects of self and suppressing or transforming those that are not so desirable. The issue of what is desirable in devotees and garments is entangled with the processes of invoking desire for Krishna and consequently the shaping of people as devotional subjects. Desire for the deity is the overarching theme of *bhakti*. This desire must be invoked within everyday routines and interactions involving a network of objects and subjects. Desire is not the result of one event or moment but is produced by a continuous mediation of interior and exterior, visible and invisible, and tangible and intangible, with subjects incorporating/excorporating entities ranging from material and emotional props/prompts in the environment to more intangible rules and norms. While the culture may indeed use rules and norms to enforce orthopraxy, what has been shown here is *how* emotions, senses, and objects extend subjects beyond their corporeal boundaries and transform them into devotees of Krishna. And how seemingly mundane activities of dressing oneself or the more specialized practices of deity dressing/dressmaking are conduits that channel the relational and binding flow of the sacred through a community.

The visual spectacle of the transcendental altar is shared and partaken by deity and devotee during *darshan*, and garments may be recycled once their life on the altar is complete. The concept of *prasad* ensures that offerings made by human hands are transformed on the altar and returned back to the congregation, thus completing the relational exchange. The value of the sacred as transcendent-but-immanent is thus maintained both through the hierarchy of the altar and through the circulation of divine substances among devotees as transmuted food, decorations, clothing, and flowers. By ingesting these offerings, devotees consume the sacred in various forms, and the benevolence of the deity (and the partaking of the divine body) is demonstrated as a shared value.

The term "efficacious intimacy" is proposed here as a means of conceptualizing embodiment and praxis in the context of devotional making and usage whereby the devotee's ability to use material and bodily resources helps to generate relationships that bind the community members with each other as well as their belief in the deity. In a global context this binding must be flexible enough to move as well as emplace devotees in different sites: to be translocally transcendent, ISKCON's practices must be movable as well as experientially compelling. As for portability of these beliefs, one could argue that part of the work of transposability was already done by Bhaktivinoda Thakur and his son Bhaktisiddhanta Saraswati through the late nineteenth century to the early twentieth century, when they helped to rationalize Gaudiya Vaishnavism and presented it in a format that could be understood by Christians. Although the message was ready, in order to make it widely disseminated, the sustained efforts of Prabhupada, the use of print technology and access to the West were required. The sustenance of beliefs and associated practices, however, does not occur simply by knowing key tenets. Instead, it requires the praxeological and phenomenological engagement of subjects as devotees. In addition, there is the necessity for "divisible" devotees to be initiated into and sustain Indic (in this case specifically Hindu Vaishnav) beliefs in caste practices through devotional living and a revitalized, Brahmanical code.

To consider how (inter)subjective experiences might emplace a devotee within a global terrain, let us turn again to the concept of ritual as emotion and sensory management and transformation through corporeal connectivity. Devotees use materials in an intentional manner but are also in turn transformed by objects. The act of performing devotion becomes its own register of intimate experience and knowledge, one that is different from the discursive and makes it possible to accept the paradox of a deity who is both immanent and transcendent—in the subject's soul as well as far away. Devotional intimacy is not a given and is not easily sustainable; the devotee incorporates the divine, whether envisioned as a material, a process, or a value, essentially by moving. The use of touch to form relationships through physical/metaphysical contact was invoked in the various sections in this monograph. For instance, *darshan* in the temple is essentially a form of visual tactility that pulls the devotee closer to the deity. Across objects and subjects, devotees placed emphasis on figuration as a means of identifying with the right, efficacious form and gaining value. Patting, handling, and pressing were common actions, and touch could be said to lubricate and animate surfaces to create contact, intimacy and relationships.

Embroidery and chanting at first seem to be two different activities whereby one practice connotes productivity and opulence and the other, redundancy and asceticism; yet both are based on accumulating value by embellishing and transforming external and internal surfaces. In both cases techniques of beads and threads bind the devotee to the practice as well as engendering hope of divine reciprocity. These practices are advantageous for the practitioner not only because they have symbolic value but also because they haptically and emotionally enact and reenact the binding and connecting of devotee to deity. Activities, such as embroidery and chanting, can be understood as techniques of spirituality, reverence, allegiance and interpreting them as efficacious forms of intimacy helps us understand these complex processes.

Touch and motion are ways of fitting and connecting actions, objects, and values together to create the subject and his or her devotional landscape. ISKCON's deities and devotees physically and metaphysically move across categories of matter and spirit, and regions and nations, as do ISKCON's devotional practices of *bhakti*. Through the devotees' use of processes, such as dressing and dressmaking, the efficacy of the sacred could be said to literally flow through the various bodies (human, social, and divine), thereby supporting a global flow of devotion-in-motion. As the various examples covered in this monograph indicate, motion and tactility accompany each other in a form of praxeological and phenomenological contact between the devout subject and the material world. When situated against a background of aesthetic, visual and tactile perception and sensitivity owing to repetitive practices and routines, motions and emotions are not isolated or quixotic but evoke a larger ethos of devotion. Most important, for devotees the efficacy of such actions renders the divine real and accessible, thereby facilitating the possibility of salvation.

References

Appadurai, Arjun. 1996. *Modernity at Large: Cultural Dimensions of Globalization.* Minneapolis: University of Minnesota Press.

Arthur, Linda B. 2000. *Undressing Religion: Commitment and Conversion from a Cross-Cultural Perspective.* Oxford: Berg/Bloomsbury Academic.

Assmann, Jan. 2011. "What's Wrong with Images?" in *Idol Anxiety*, eds. Josh Ellenbogen and Aaron Tugendhaft. Stanford, CA: Stanford University Press, pp. 19–31.

Babb, Lawrence. 1981. "Glancing: Visual Interaction in Hinduism," *Journal of Anthropological Research*, vol. 37, no. 4, pp. 387–401.

Banerjee, Mukulika and Daniel Miller. 2003. *The Sari.* Oxford: Berg.

Bayly, Christopher Alan. 1986. "The Origins of Swadeshi (Home Industry): Cloth and Indian Society, 1700–1930," in *The Social Life of Things: Commodities in Cultural Perspective*, ed. Arjun Appadurai. Cambridge: Cambridge University Press, pp. 285–321.

Bernardi, Luciano, Peter Sleight, Gabrielle Bandinelli, Simone Cencetti, Lamberto Fattorini, Johanna Wdowczyc-Szulc, and Alfonso Lagi. 2001. "Effect of Rosary Prayer and Yoga Mantras on Autonomic Cardiovascular Rhythms: Comparative Study," *British Medical Journal*, vol. 323, no. 7327, pp. 1446–1449.

Berthoz, Alain. 2000. *The Brain's Sense of Movement.* Cambridge: Harvard University Press.

Bhatia, Varuni. 2017. *Unforgetting Chaitanya: Vaishnavism and Cultures of Devotion in Colonial Bengal.* New York: Oxford University Press.

Bhatti, Shaila, and Christopher Pinney. 2011. "Optic-Clash: Modes of Visuality in India," in *A Companion to the Anthropology of India*, ed. Isabella Clark-Deces. Hoboken, NJ: Wiley-Blackwell, pp. 225–240.

Bourdieu, Pierre. 1990. *The Logic of Practice.* Stanford: Stanford University Press.

Brett, David. 2005. *Rethinking Decoration: Pleasure and Ideology in the Visual Arts.* Cambridge: Cambridge University Press.

Bromley, David, and Larry Shinn, eds. 1989. *Krishna Consciousness in the West.* Plainsboro: Associated University Presses.

Brooks, Charles R. 1989. *The Hare Krishnas in India.* New Delhi: Motilal Banarsidass.

Brooks, Charles R. 1990. "Hare Krishna, Radhe Shyam: The Cross-Cultural Dynamics of Mystical Emotions in Brindaban," in *Divine Passions: The Social Construction of Emotion in India*, ed. Owen Lynch. Berkeley and Los Angeles: University of California Press, pp. 262–285.

Brosius, Christiane. 2011. "The Multiple Bodies of the Bride. Ritualising 'World Class' at Elite Weddings in Urban India," in *Images of the Body in India*, eds. Axel Michaels and Christoph Wulf. New Delhi: Routledge, pp. 261–279.

Brosius, Christiane. 2010. "A Spiritual Mega-Experience: The Akshardham Cultural Complex," in *India's Middle Class: New Forms of Urban Leisure, Consumption and Prosperity*. New Delhi and Oxford: Routledge, pp. 143–258.

Brown, Sara. 2012. "Every Word Is a Song, Every Step Is a Dance: Participation, Agency and Communal Bliss in Hare Krishna Festival Kirtan." Doctoral Thesis.

Bryant, Edwin, and Maria Ekstrand, eds. 2004. *The Hare Krishna Movement: The Postcharismatic Fate of a Religious Transplant.* New York: Columbia University Press.

Brydon, Anne, and Sandra Niessen, eds. 1998. *Consuming Fashion: Adorning the Transnational Body.* New York: Berg/Bloomsbury Academic.

Buck-Morss, Susan. 1992. "Aesthetics and Anaesthetics: Walter Benjamin's Artwork Essay Reconsidered," *October*, vol. 62, pp. 3–41.

Cannadine, David. 2002. *Ornamentalism: How the British Saw Their Empire.* Oxford and London: Oxford University Press.

Codell, Julie, ed. 2011. *Power and Resistance: The Delhi Coronation Durbars 1877, 1903, 1911.* New Delhi: Mapin Publishing and Alkazi Collection of Photography.

Cohn, Bernard S. 1987. *An Anthropologist among the Historians and Other Essays.* Delhi: Oxford University Press.

Cohn, Bernard S. 1989. "Cloth, Clothes and Colonialism: India in the Nineteenth Century," in *Cloth and Human Experience*, eds. Annette Weiner and Jane Schneider. Washington, D.C.: Smithsonian, pp. 303–353.

Coomaraswamy, Ananda K., 1939. "Ornament," *Art Bulletin*, no. 21, pp. 1–19.

Csordas, Thomas J. 1990. "Embodiment as a Paradigm for Anthropology," *Ethos*, vol. 18, no. 1, pp. 5–47.

Csordas, Thomas J., ed. 1994. *Embodiment and Experience: The Existential Ground of Culture and Self.* New York: Cambridge University Press.

Csordas, Thomas J. 1997. *The Sacred Self: A Cultural Phenomenology of Charismatic Healing.* Berkeley and Los Angeles: University of California Press.

Csordas, Thomas J., ed. 2009. *Transnational Transcendence: Essays on Religion and Globalization.* Berkeley and Los Angeles: University of California Press.

Das, Madhusevita. 2005. *Darsana: Krishna Meditation.* Los Angeles: Bhaktivedanta Book Trust.

Dasa, Hayagriva. 1985. *The Hare Krishna Explosion: The Birth of Krishna Consciousness in America 1966–69.* Santa Fe, NM: Palace Press.

Davis, Richard H. 1997. "Living Images," in *Lives of Indian Images*, Richard H. Davis. Princeton, NJ: Princeton University Press, pp. 15–50.

De Abreu, Maria Jose A. 2008. "Goose Bumps All Over: Breath, Media, and Tremor," *Social Text 96*, vol. 26, no. 3, pp. 59–78.

Dehejia, Vidya. 2009. *The Body Adorned: Dissolving Boundaries between Sacred and Profane in India's Art.* New York; Columbia University Press.

Dimock, Edward C. Jr. 1999. *Caitanya Caritamrta of Krsnadasa Kaviraja: A Translation and Commentary.* Harvard Oriental Series, vol. 56. Cambridge: Harvard University Press.

Durkheim, Emile. 2008 (1912). "The Elementary Forms of Religious Life," in *A Reader in the Anthropology of Religion*, ed. Michael Lambek. Oxford: Blackwell Publishing Ltd., pp. 34–47.

Dwyer, Rachel. 2004. "International Hinduism: The Swaminarayan Sect," in *South Asians in the Diaspora: Histories and Religious Traditions*, eds. Knut Jacobsen and Pratap Kumar. Leiden: Brill, pp. 180–199.

Dwyer, Graham, and Richard Cole, eds. 2007. *The Hare Krishna Movement: Forty Years of Chant and Change.* London: I. B. Tauris.

Eaton, Richard M. 1993. *The Rise of Islam and the Bengal Frontier*, 1204–1760. Berkeley and Los Angeles: University of California Press.

Eck, Diana. 1981. *Darsan: Seeing the Divine Image in India.* Chambersburg, PA: Anima Books.

Entwistle, Joanne, and Elizabeth Wilson, eds. 2001. *Body Dressing.* New York: Berg/Bloomsbury Academic.

Fleming, Benjamin, and Richard Mann, eds. 2014. *Material Culture in Asian Religions: Text, Image, Object.* London: Routledge.

Flood, Finbarr B. 2009. "Cultural Cross-dressing," in *Objects of Translation: Material Culture and Medieval "Hindu-Muslim" Encounter*, Finbarr B. Flood. Princeton, NJ: Princeton University Press, pp. 61–286.

Foucault, Michel. 1988. "Technologies of the Self," in *Technologies of the Self: A Seminar with Michel Foucault*, eds. Luther H. Martin, Huck Gutman, and Patrick Hutton. Amherst: University of Massachusetts Press, pp. 16–49.

Fuller, Christopher. 2004. *The Camphor Flame: Popular Hinduism and Society in India.* Princeton, NJ: Princeton University Press.

Fuller, Jason. 2003. "Re-Membering the Tradition: Bhaktivinoda Thakura's Sajjanatosani and the Construction of a Middle-Class Vaisnava Sampradaya in Nineteenth-Century Bengal," in *Hinduism in Public and Private*, ed. Anthony Copley New Delhi: Oxford University Press, pp. 173–210.

Fuller, Jason. 2005a. "Religion, Class, and Power: Bhaktivinode Thakur and the Transformation of Religious Authority among the Gaudiya Vaisnavas in Nineteenth-century Bengal." Doctoral Thesis.

Fuller, Jason. 2005b. "Reading, Writing and Reclaiming: Bhaktivinoda Thakura and the Modernization of Gaudiya Vaishnavism," *Journal of Vaishnav Studies*, vol. 13, no. 2, pp. 75–94.

Ganguly, Anil. 1979. *Fine Arts in Ancient India.* New Delhi: Abhinav Publications.

Gell, Alfred. 1992. "The Technology of Enchantment and the Enchantment of Technology," in *Anthropology, Art, and Aesthetics*, eds. Jeremy Coote and Anthony Shelton. Oxford: Oxford University Press, pp. 40–63.

Gell, Alfred. 1998. *Art and Agency: An Anthropological Theory.* Oxford: Clarendon.

Ghosh, Pika. 2005. *Temple to Love: Architecture and Devotion in Seventeenth-Century Bengal.* Bloomington: Indiana University Press.

Gonda, Jan. 1975. *Selected Studies: Indo-European linguistics, Volume II.* Leiden: Brill.

Gosvami, Rupa. 2003. *The Bhaktirasamritasindhu of Rupa Gosvamin*, transl. David Haberman. New Delhi: IGNCA and Motilal Banarsidass.

Goswami, Gopala Bhatta. 1997. *Sat Kriya Sara Dipika.* Mayapur: The Bhaktivedanta Academy.

Goswami, Tamal Krishna. 2012. *A Living Theology of Krishna Bhakti: The Essential Teachings of A. C. Bhaktivedanta Swami Prabhupada.* Oxford and New York: Oxford University Press.

Gowlland, Geoffrey. 2011. "The 'Matière à Penser' Approach to Material Culture: Objects, Subjects and the Materiality of the Self," *Journal of Material Culture*, vol. 16, no. 3, pp. 337–343.

Gupta, Charu S. 1996. *Zardozi, Glittering Gold Embroidery.* New Delhi: Abhinav Publications.

Guy, Ali, Maura Banim, and Eileen Green, eds. 2001. *Through the Wardrobe: Women's Relationships with Their Clothes.* New York: Berg/Bloomsbury Academic.

Hacker, Katherine. 2004. "Dressing Lord Jagannatha in Silk: Cloth, Clothes, and Status," *Journal of Social Sciences*, vol. 8, no. 2, pp. 113–127.

Hawley, John S. 1995. "The Nirgun/Sagun Distinction in Early Manuscript Anthologies of Hindu Devotion," in *Bhakti Religion in North India: Community Identity and Political Action*, ed. David Lorenzen. Albany: State University of New York Press, pp. 160–180.

Hawley, John S. 2015. *A Storm of Songs: India and the Idea of the Bhakti Movement.* Cambridge: Harvard University Press.

Hobsbawm, Eric and Terence Ranger. 1983. *The Invention of Tradition.* Cambridge: Cambridge University Press.

Holdrege, Barbara. 2014. *Bhakti and Embodiment: Fashioning Divine Bodies and Devotional Bodies in Krsna Bhakti.* London and New York: Routledge.

Hume, Lynne. 2013. *The Religious Life of Dress: Global Fashion and Faith.* London and New York; Bloomsbury.

Inden, Ronald B. 1976. *Marriage and Rank in Bengali Culture: A History of Caste and Clan in Middle Period Bengal.* Berkeley and Los Angeles: University of California Press.

Inden, Ronald B. 1986. "Orientalist Constructions of India," *Modern Asian Studies*, vol. 20, no. 3, pp. 401–446.

Inden, Ronald B., and Ralph W. Nicholas. 1977. *Kinship in Bengali Culture.* Chicago: University of Chicago Press.

Jacobsen, Knut A., Michel Aktor, and Kristina Myrvold, eds. 2015. *Objects of Worship in South Asian Religions: Forms, Practices and Meanings.* London and New York: Routledge.

Jain, Kajri. 2007. *Gods in the Bazaar: The Economies of Indian Calendar Art.* Durham, NC: Duke University Press.

Jeon, Eun J. 2014. "Form Empowered by Touch, Movement, and Emotion," in *Fashion Design for Living*, ed. Alison Gwilt. London: Routledge.

Kant, Immanuel. 2007 (1790). *Critique of Judgement* (*Kritik der Urteilskraft*), transl. Nicholas Walker. Oxford and New York: Oxford University Press.

Kawlra, Aarti. 2005. "Kanchipuram Sari: Design for Auspiciousness," *Design Issues*, vol. 21, no. 4, pp. 54–67.

Keane, Webb. 2003. "Semiotics and the Social Analysis of Material Things," *Language & Communication*, vol. 23, no. 3–4, pp. 409–425.

King, Anna S. 2012. "Krishna's Prasadam: 'Eating Our Way Back to Godhead'," *Material Religion*, vol. 8, no. 4, pp. 440–465.

King, Richard. 1999. *Orientalism and Religion: Post-Colonial Theory, India and "The Mystic East".* New York: Routledge.

Kipling, John L. 1891. *Beast and Man in India: A Popular Sketch of Indian Animals in Their Relations with the People.* London and New York: Macmillan and Co.

Kratky, Jan. 2012. "Cognition, Material Culture and Religious Ritual," *Diskus*, vol. 13, pp. 49–62.

Küchler, Susanne, and Graeme Were, eds. 2005. *The Art of Clothing: A Pacific Experience.* London: University College London.

Laine, James. 2010. "Mind and Mood in the Study of Religion," *Religion*, vol. 40, no. 4, pp. 239–249.

Lemonnier, Pierre. 1992. *Elements for an Anthropology of Technology.* Ann Arbor: University of Michigan.

Leroi-Gourhan, Andre. 1993 (1964). *Gesture and Speech.* Boston: MIT Press.

Leslie, Julie. 1993. "The Significance of Dress for the Orthodox Hindu Woman," in *Dress and Gender: Making and Meaning in Cultural Contexts*, eds. Ruth Barnes and Joanne Eicher. Oxford: Berg, pp. 198–213.

Lipner, Julius J. 1994. *Hindus: Their Religious Beliefs and Practices.* London and New York: Routledge.

Lipner, Julius J. 2006. "The Rise of 'Hinduism'; or, How to Invent a World Religion with Only Moderate Success," *International Journal of Hindu Studies*, vol. 10, no. 1, pp. 91–104.

Lipner, Julius J. 2017. *Hindu Images and Their Worship with Special Reference to Vaisnavism: A Philosophical-Theological Inquiry.* London and New York: Routledge.

Loos, Adolf. 1998 (1908). "Ornament and Crime," in Adolf Loos, *Ornament and Crime*: *Selected Essays*, transl. Michael Mitchell. Riverside, CA: Ariadne Press, pp. 167–176.

Luchesi, Brigitte. 2015. "Jhankis. 'Living Images' as Objects of worship in Himachal Pradesh," in *Objects of Worship in South Asian Religions: Forms, practices and meanings*, eds. Knutt A. Jacobsen, Mikael Aktor and Kristina Myrvold. Oxon: Routledge, pp. 35–50.

Lutgendorf, Philip. 1991. *The Life of a Text: Performing the Ramcaritmanas of Tulsidas.* Berkeley and Los Angeles: University of California Press.

Lyons, Tryna. 2004. *The Artists of Nathdwara: The Practice of Painting in Rajasthan.* Bloomington: Indiana University Press; Ahmedabad: Mapin.

Lyons, Tryna. 2009. "Terra Ephemera: The Case of a New Goddess in Bengal," *Artibus Asia*, vol. 69, no. 2, pp. 259–294.

Madan, T. N. 1985. "Concerning the Categories Subha and Sudha in Hindu Culture: An Exploratory Essay," in *Purity and Auspiciousness in Indian Society*, eds. John Carman and Frederique Marglin. Leiden: Brill, pp. 11–29.

Mann, Richard. 2014. "Material Culture and the Study of Hinduism and Buddhism," *Religion Compass*, vol. 8, no. 8, pp. 264–273.

Marriott, McKim. 1976. "Hindu Transactions; Diversity without Dualism," in *Transaction and Meaning: Directions in the Anthropology of Exchange and Symbolic Behavior*, ed. Bruce Kapferer. Philadelphia: Institute for the Study of Human Issues, pp. 109–142.

Marriott, McKim. 1990. *India through Hindu Categories.* London: Sage Publications.

Marriott, McKim, and Ronald Inden. 1977. "Toward an Ethnosociology of South Asian Caste Systems," in *The New Wind: Changing Identities in South Asia*, ed. Kenneth David. The Hague: Mouton Publishers, pp. 227–238.

Mauss, Marcel. 2006 (1935). "Techniques of the Body," in *Techniques, Technology and Civilisation*, ed. Nathan Schlanger. New York: Berghahn Books, pp. 77–95.

McGowan, Abigail. 2009. *Crafting the Nation in Colonial India.* New York: Palgrave Macmillan.

Merleau-Ponty, Maurice. 2012 (1945). *Phenomenology of Perception.* London: Routledge.

Miles, Margaret. 1998. "Image," in *Critical Terms for Religious Studies*, ed. Mark Taylor. Chicago: University of Chicago Press, pp. 160–172.

Miller, Daniel. 1994. "Style and Ontology," in *Consumption and Identity*, ed. Jonathan Friedman. Oxfordshire: Taylor & Francis, pp. 71–96.

Mohan, Urmila. 2015. "Dressing God: Clothing as Religious Subjectivity in a Hindu Group," in *The Social Life of Materials: Studies in Materials and Society*, eds. Adam Drazin and Susanne Küchler. London and New York: Bloomsbury, pp. 137–152.

Mohan, Urmila. 2016. "From Prayer Beads to the Mechanical Counter: The Negotiation of Chanting Practices within a Hindu Group," *Archives de Sciences Sociales des Religions*, vol. 174, pp. 191–212.

Mohan, Urmila. 2017a. "Clothing as a Technology of Enchantment: Gaze and Glaze in Hindu Garments," *Magic, Ritual, and Witchcraft*, vol. 12, no. 1, pp. 225–244.

Mohan, Urmila. 2017b. "When Krishna Wore a Kimono: Deity Clothing as Rupture and Inefficacy," in *The Material Culture of Failure: When Things Do Wrong*, eds. Timothy Carroll, David Jeevendrampillai, Aaron Parkhurst, and Julie Shackelford. London and New York: Bloomsbury, pp. 39–55.

Mohan, Urmila and Laurence Douny, eds. 2020. *The Material Subject: Rethinking Subjects Through Objects and Praxis.* London: Bloomsbury.

Mohan, Urmila, and Jean-Pierre Warnier. 2017. "Editorial: Marching the Devotional Subject: The Bodily-and-Material Cultures of Religion," *Journal of Material Culture*, vol. 22, no. 4, pp. 369–384.

Monier-Williams, Monier. 2005 (1872). *A Sanskrit-English Dictionary.* New Delhi: Motilal Banarsidass.

Morgan, David. 1998. *Visual Piety: A History and Theory of Popular Religious Images.* Berkeley and Los Angeles: University of California Press.

Morgan, David. 2010. "The Material Culture of Lived Religions: Visuality and Embodiment," *Mind and Matter: Selected Papers of Nordik Conference 2009. Studies in Art History*, vol. 41, ed. Johanna Vakkari. Helsinki: Society of Art History, pp. 14–31.

Naji, Myriem, and Laurence Douny. 2009. "Editorial: Special Issue on 'Making' and 'Doing' the Material World," *Journal of Material Culture*, vol. 14, no. 4, pp. 411–432.

Nanda, Meera. 2011. *The God Market: How Globalization Is Making India More Hindu.* New York: Monthly Review Press.

Nandy, Ashis. 1983. *The Intimate Enemy: Loss and Recovery of Self Under Colonialism.* Delhi: Oxford University Press.

Narayanan, Vasudha. 2003. "Embodied Cosmologies: Sights of Piety, Sites of Power," *Journal of the American Academy of Religion*, vol. 71, no. 3, pp. 495–520.

Niessen, Sandra, ed. 2003. *Re-Orienting Fashion: The Globalization of Asian Dress.* New York: Berg/Bloomsbury Academic.

Nye, Malory. 2001. *Multiculturalism and Minority Religions in Britain: Krishna Consciousness, Religious Freedom and the Politics of Location.* Richmond, UK: Curzon.

Packert, Cynthia. 2010. *The Art of Loving Krishna: Ornamentation and Devotion.* Bloomington: Indiana University Press.

Paulicelli, Eugenia, and Hazel Clark, eds. 2009. *The Fabric of Cultures: Fashion, Identity and Globalization.* London: Routledge.

Pinney, Christopher. 1997. *Camera Indica: The Social Life of Indian Photographs.* Chicago: University of Chicago Press.

Pinney, Christopher. 1999. "On Living in the Kal(i)yug: Notes from Nagda, Madhya Pradesh," *Contributions to Indian Sociology*, vol. 33, no. 1–2, pp. 77–106.

Pinney, Christopher. 2004. *"Photos of the Gods": The Printed Image and Political Struggle in India.* London: Reaktion Books.

Pinney, Christopher. 2009. "Camerawork as Technical Practice in Colonial India," in *Material Powers: Cultural Studies, History and the Material Turn*, eds. Tony Bennett and Patrick Joyce New York: Routledge, pp. 145–170.

Prabhupada, A. C. 1983. *The Science of Self Realization.* Los Angeles: Bhaktivedanta Book Trust.

Prabhupada, A. C. 1986. *The Bhagavad Gita as It Is.* Los Angeles: Bhaktivedanta Book Trust.

Prentiss, Karen P. 1999. *The Embodiment of Bhakti.* Oxford and New York: Oxford University Press.

Ramaswamy, Sumathi. 2010. *The Goddess and the Nation: Mapping Mother India.* Durham, NC: Duke University Press.

Rochford, E. Burke. 1985. *Hare Krishna in America.* New Brunswick, NJ: Rutgers University Press.

Rochford, E. Burke. 2007. *Hare Krishna Transformed.* New York and London: New York University Press.

Sander, Ake, and Clemens Cavallin. 2015. "Hinduism Meets the Global Order: The 'Easternization' of the West," in *The Changing World Religion Map. Sacred Places, Identities, Practices and Politics*, Vol. III, ed. Stanley D. Brunn. New York and London: Springer, pp. 1743–1766.

Sandhu, Arti. 2015. *Indian Fashion: Tradition, Innovation, Style.* London and New York: Bloomsbury Academic.

Sarbadhikary, Sukanya. 2015. *The Place of Devotion: Siting and Experiencing Divinity in Bengal-Vaishnavism.* Berkeley and Los Angeles: University of California Press.

Sardella, Ferdinando. 2013. *Modern Hindu Personalism: The History, Life, and Thought of Bhaktisiddhanta Sarasvati.* Oxford and New York: Oxford University Press.

Sarkar, Sumit. 1997. *Writing Social History.* New Delhi: Oxford University Press, pp. 282–357.

Schilder, Paul. 1950 (1935). *The Image and Appearance of the Human Body.* London: Routledge.

Schwartz, Susan. 2004. *Rasa: Performing the Divine in India.* New York: Columbia University Press.

Sharma, Arvind. 2011. *Hinduism as a Missionary Religion.* Albany: State University of New York Press.

Sharma, B. G. 2004. *Krishna Art Postcard Book.* San Rafael, CA: Mandala Publishing Group.

Strasdin, Kate. 2012. "Empire Dressing—The Design & Realization of Queen Alexandra's Coronation Gown," *Journal of Design History*, vol. 25, no. 2, pp. 155–170.

Strathern, Andrew. 1996. *Body Thoughts.* Ann Arbor: University of Michigan Press.

Sugirtharajah, Sharada. 2003. "Max Muller: Mobilizing Texts and Managing Hinduism," in *Imagining Hinduism: A Postcolonial Perspective*, Sharada Sugirtharajah. London and New York: Routledge, pp. 38–73.

Tarlo, Emma. 1996. *Clothing Matters: Dress and Identity in India.* London: C. Hurst.

Tripurari, Swami B. V., and B. G. Sharma. 2005. *Form of Beauty: The Krishna Art of B. G. Sharma.* San Rafael, CA: Mandala Publishing Group.

Tu, Rachel. 2009. "Dressing the Nation: India Cinema Costume and the Making of a National Fashion 1947–1957," in *The Fabric of Cultures: Fashion, Identity and Globalization*, Eugenia Paulicelli and Hazel Clark, eds. London: Routledge, pp. 28–40.

Valpey, Kenneth. 2006. *Attending Krsna's Image: Caitanya Vaisnava Murti-seva as Devotional Truth.* London: Routledge.

Vande Berg, Travis, and Fred Kniss. 2008. "Iskcon and Immigrants: The Rise, Decline, and Rise Again of a New Religious Movement," *The Sociological Quarterly*, no. 49, pp. 79–104.

Varma, K. M. 1970. *The Indian Technique of Clay Modelling.* Santiniketan: Proddu.

Vatsyayan, Kapila. 1996. *Bharata, The Natyasastra.* New Delhi: Sahitya Academy.

Waghorne, Joanne, Norman Cutler, and Vasudha Narayanan, eds. 1985. *Gods of Flesh, Gods of Stone: The Embodiment of Divinity in India.* New York: Columbia University Press.

Waghorne, Joanne Punzo. 1994. *The Raja's Magic Clothes: Re-Visioning Kingship and Divinity in England's India.* University Park: Pennsylvania State University Press.

Waghorne, Joanne Punzo. 2004. *The Diaspora of the Gods: Modern Hindu Temples in an Urban Middle-Class World.* New York: Oxford University Press.

Warnier, Jean-Pierre. 2007. *The Pot-King: The Body and Technologies of Power.* Leiden: Brill.

Warnier, Jean-Pierre. 2009. "Technology as Efficacious Action on Objects ... and Subjects," *Journal of Material Culture*, vol. 14, no. 4, pp. 459–470.

Wilkinson-Weber, Clare. 2014. *Fashioning Bollywood: The Making and Meaning of Hindi Film Costume.* London and New York: Bloomsbury Academic.

Zaidman, Nurit. 1997. "When the Deities Are Asleep: Processes of Change in an American Hare Krishna Temple," *Journal of Contemporary Religion*, vol. 12, no. 3, pp. 335–352.